Creativity in Secondary Education

Martin Fautley
Jonathan Savage

LearningMatters

First published in 2007 by Learning Matters Ltd

British Library Cataloguing in Publication Data
A CIP record for this book is available from the British Library.

ISBN 978 1 84445 073 2

Cover design by Topics – The Creative Partnership
Project management by Deer Park Productions, Tavistock, Devon
Typeset by PDQ Typesetting Ltd
Printed and bound in Great Britain by Cromwell Press Ltd, Trowbridge, Wiltshire

Learning Matters Ltd
33 Southernhay East
Exeter EX1 1NX
Tel: 01392 215560
info@learningmatters.co.uk
www.learningmatters.co.uk

Achieving
QTS

Creativity in
Sec

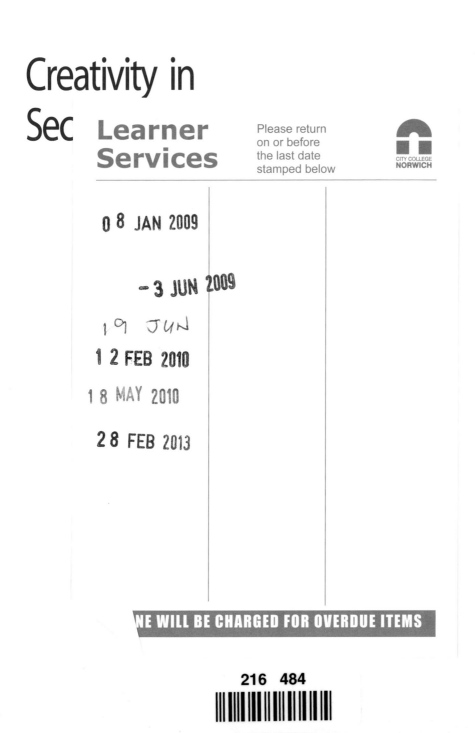

Contents

The authors

Martin Fautley

Martin Fautley is a Senior Lecturer in Education at the University of Central England in Birmingham. For many years he was a school teacher in the Midlands before undertaking doctoral research at the University of Cambridge. His research interests encompass theoretical and practical issues concerning creative processes in schools and how teachers can help to foster these.

Jonathan Savage

Jonathan Savage is a Senior Lecturer in Education at the Institute of Education, Manchester Metropolitan University. Until 2001 he was Head of Music at Debenham High School, an 11–16 comprehensive school in rural Suffolk. He is also Managing Director of UCan.tv (**www.ucan.tv**) a not-for-profit company which produces engaging educational software.

1
Setting the scene:
creativity in secondary education

By the end of this chapter you should:

- **have thought about creativity, and what it means to be creative;**
- **have considered views of learning and how the notion of creativity sits within these;**
- **have reflected on the place of creativity within your specialist subject;**
- **have considered the role of creativity within the National Curriculum.**

This chapter will help you to meet the following Professional Standards for QTS:
Q1, Q2, Q6, Q7, Q8, Q9, Q10, Q15, Q18, Q22, Q25

Introduction

Creativity is an important concept in education and elsewhere, and it is hard to imagine it being seen as anything other than a positive attribute of individuals and institutions alike. Indeed, arguing against creativity in schools would seem to be like arguing against 'motherhood and apple pie'. But if creativity is universally acknowledged to be a good thing, it ought to be straightforward to define what it is.

PRACTICAL TASK PRACTICAL TASK **PRACTICAL TASK** PRACTICAL TASK **PRACTICAL TASK**

Have a go now – define creativity. Compose a sentence that begins 'creativity is...'

Maybe you found this slightly more problematic than you first thought? Or maybe you produced a perfectly usable definition of creativity which encompasses all possible outcomes – whichever you managed (or didn't!), let us now consider what others have written on the topic, and arrive at definitions which will be of use to us in terms of academic discourse, have meaning in day-to-day work in the classroom, and that we can take forward into the rest of this book.

Creativity – is it magic?

To go back to basics, creativity involves creation, and creation involves creating something:

> If we take seriously the dictionary definition of creation, to 'bring into being or form out of nothing', creativity seems to be not only unintelligible, but strictly impossible. No craftsman or engineer ever made an artefact from nothing. And sorcerers (or their apprentices) who conjure brooms and buckets out of thin air do so not by any intelligible means, but by occult wizardry. The 'explanation' of creativity thus reduces to either denial or magic. (Boden, 1990, p2)

And we are not going to deny that creativity exists or suggest that you need to be a Harry Potter to do it! So, if the notion of creativity implies that something is being created, what is going on? To 'do' something in normal speech usually involves some form of activity, mental and/or physical. This 'doing' also implies a *process*, and the notion of a *creative process* is one which figures significantly in the literature.

Breaking down into stages

Research into creativity was undertaken for the most part by psychologists in the first instance; more recently educational researchers, social scientists, artificial intelligence researchers and management consultants have also become involved. Many of these accounts draw on an early piece of research undertaken in the 1920s by Wallas (1926), who broke down the creative process into four stages:

Preparation   Incubation   Illumination   Verification

The first stage, *preparation*, represents the consideration of an issue, which involves getting ready for the next stage too. This is followed by *incubation*, which is defined as a period of time where the issue and its ramifications are considered, mulled over and thought about. *Illumination* involves arriving at a point of realisation where a solution presents itself or becomes apparent. Finally *verification* involves some form of testing of that which has happened.

Even after the intervening years, the four stages of the Wallas model still appear to be logical in terms of a sequence of events, and show

> ... *a continuous process, with a beginning, middle, and end of its own.*
> (Vernon, 1970, p91)

The four stages are of use in the classroom as they allow us to consider how a creative activity can be presented to our pupils. We will look later on at how you the teacher can plan for this to happen in your lessons.

Convergent, divergent and lateral thinking

Another piece of research, from later in the twentieth century, is also of concern in our discussion here. Guilford (1967) in his 'structure of intellect' model proposed that there are a number of different mental factors or abilities. According to this model there are two kinds of productive abilities, *convergent* and *divergent*. Convergent thinking moves in a linear fashion towards a fixed answer, whereas in divergent thinking there may be no fixed answer, no specified linear route to a predetermined ending, and so the thinker has considerable latitude. Divergent thinking seems particularly apposite to creativity. Closely related to it is *lateral thinking*, a term developed by de Bono, and often to be found in schools associated with his 'six hats' notion (de Bono, 1985) of developing pupil thinking skills. Divergent thinking deliberately moves away from straightforward approaches to problem-solving, and allows the possibility of novel outcomes being generated. For our consideration of creativity, it seems likely that the notion of divergent thinking is an area that we would wish to promote.

Boden: P- and H-creativity

Creativity is seen by some as being a 'special' facility. This is often called the *trait* theory of creativity and says that certain individuals have a tendency towards creativity. This work arose in the 1950s. However, in common with most contemporary commentators, we do not see it that way. For us – and, we hope, for you too – creativity is a faculty which we believe is present in all the pupils we teach, and which is possible to develop. After all, *we are all, or can be, creative to some degree* (QCA, 2004, p9). While we know Mozart had composed a lot of music by the time he was 11, child prodigies are a separate issue, and although you may have one or more in your school, our concern is with *all* the pupils in *all* our classes. This means that we need to think of creativity from what we might call an 'everyday' perspective. So, each time a child paints a picture, comes up with a new idea, plays a new arrangement of notes on a xylophone, thinks of a new way of assembling their science experiment, makes a new construction with Lego bricks or a myriad of other everyday creative acts, they can be said to be being creative, not along the lines of composing a Mozart symphony, but in a smaller, more personal way. In her writings, Margaret Boden draws a distinction between everyday creativity, which she terms *psychological* in the sense of having occurred to an individual, and those ideas which, although coming into being in the same fashion, also have *historical* importance beyond that of the immediate. These she designates as P-creative and H-creative:

> *If Mary Smith has an idea which she could not have had before, her idea is P-creative – no matter how many people have had the same idea already. The historical sense applies to ideas that are fundamentally novel with respect to the whole of human history. Mary Smith's surprising idea is H-creative if no one has ever had the idea before her.* (Boden, 1990, p32)

This distinction between two different types of creativity is important, as it allows for the individual to produce something which is new for them, but not necessarily new for the world. Anna Craft is referring to a similar idea when she writes of:

> *... the kind of creativity which guides choices and route-finding in everyday life, or what I have come to term 'little c' creativity.* (Craft, 2000, p3)

We shall return to the notion of creativity for everyone throughout this book, particularly in Chapter 7 when we discuss inclusion.

What we have discovered:

- **Creativity involves doing something.**
- **This something is new for the doer, but maybe not entirely novel in historical terms.**
- **Creativity is not something only done by 'special' people.**
- **You, and everyone in your class, can be creative.**
- **Everyday creativity is valid.**

Creativity for every subject

Another misconception that we need to deal with straight away is that creativity is only the rightful province of the Arts. Creativity can be found in all areas of the school curriculum, and beyond. As a science teacher observed.

> *... creativity always goes hand-in-hand with art, drama, dance, music, [but] it isn't just about the arts, so to speak, it's about being creative with the curriculum, rather than just using the 'arty-farty' subjects.* (Fautley, 2005, p12)

This point is made in the National Curriculum handbook (QCA, 1999, pp11–12) where the importance of creativity across all subjects is discussed.

> *By providing rich and varied contexts for pupils to acquire, develop and apply a broad range of knowledge, understanding and skills, the curriculum should enable pupils to think creatively and critically, to solve problems and to make a difference for the better. It should give them the opportunity to become creative, innovative, enterprising and capable of leadership to equip them for their future lives as workers and citizens.*

The QCA has also recognised the importance of creativity across the curriculum, and their *Creativity: find it, promote it!* (QCA, 2004) materials observe that:

> *pupils who are encouraged to think creatively and independently become:*
>
> - *more interested in discovering things for themselves;*
> - *more open to new ideas;*
> - *keen to work with others to explore ideas;*
> - *willing to work beyond lesson time when pursuing an idea or vision.*
>
> *As a result, their pace of learning, levels of achievement and self-esteem increase.* (QCA, 2004, p9)

So, creativity is relevant across the curriculum and impacts on a number of other areas.

Creativity as active process

Let us return now to our search for a definition of creativity. We have decided that creativity involves *doing*, in other words *action*. This means that creativity is an *active process*.

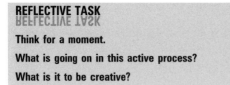

REFLECTIVE TASK

Think for a moment.

What is going on in this active process?

What is it to be creative?

Hopefully you returned to our discussion and decided that creativity involves some form of mental activity. This is not all though – the dancer uses her body *and* her mind. Mental and physical processes are involved, as they are in many spheres of creative activity. But the thing that lies at the heart of this process is a *decision-making process* which involves choosing different paths at certain key points. It is this which is the key to creativity. Divergent thinking; thinking 'outside the box'; 'blue skies' thinking – all these are terms which imply that something out of the ordinary is taking place. This difference can be attributed to decisions which are being taken – and taken, in many cases, deliberately. There can be chance examples of creative decision-making, but in the classroom you will not want to wait for these but pursue a more purposeful course aimed at producing this type of thinking. Such decision making processes can result in what Wallas (1926) would have called *illumination*, or what others would call a *Eureka moment*. They are the result of a way of thinking – 'outside the box' – which does not involve a tried-and-tested response but instead goes off in a different direction, it *diverges* from the expected.

In Figure 1.1 the straightforward linear response moves directly from the starting point to the end, with no deviation from the straight and narrow; there will obviously be numerous occasions in school when this linear response is the one which is required. The divergent response is shown as going off in different directions, and taking a broader path to the endpoint. In this way of thinking the journey is as important, if not more so, than the destination.

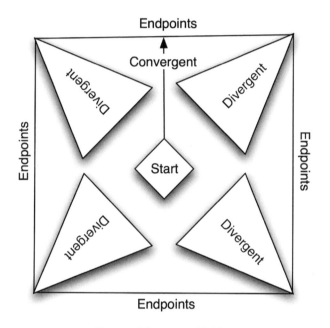

Fig. 1.1. Divergent thinking

Characteristics of creativity

To arrive, then, at a working definition for creativity we need to consider the things we have discussed so far. A recent definition of creativity is provided in the National Advisory Committee on Creative and Cultural Education (NACCCE) report (NACCCE, 1999), where creativity is discussed in terms of four characteristics:

> *First, they always involve thinking or behaving imaginatively. Second, overall this imaginative activity is purposeful: that is, it is directed to achieving an objective. Third, these processes must generate something original. Fourth, the outcome must be of value in relation to the objective.* (NACCCE, 1999, p29)

This provides us with a useful set of descriptors for the characteristics of creativity. This does not mean that we can only consider creativity to be judged in terms of its usefulness:

> *Creativity should be defined by the novelty of its products, not by their usefulness, value, profitability, beauty, and so on. What is not useful now may become useful*

in a distant future. Even if it is never applied for the benefit of mankind it may, in principle, be called creative ... (Smith, 2005, p294)

The notion of 'imagination' can be problematic too – and we shall be exploring this later!

So, bearing in mind all of the above, we are now in a position to produce our own working definition of creativity (see Figure 1.2):

Creativity ...
- **involves mental processes;**
- **can involve action;**
- **is within a domain;**
- **is purposeful;**
- **is novel (to the individual – 'everyday' creativity).**

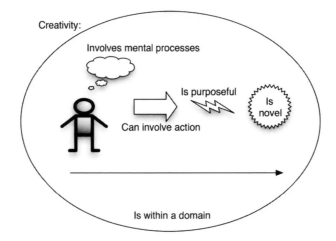

Fig. 1.2. Creativity

This gives us something with which to proceed! It covers all of the main factors we have described so far and allows for everyday creativity – the sort you are most likely to see in your classroom – to be recognised and valued.

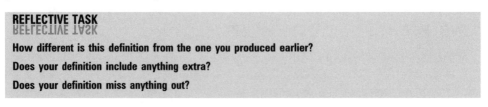

REFLECTIVE TASK

How different is this definition from the one you produced earlier?

Does your definition include anything extra?

Does your definition miss anything out?

One of the reasons for establishing a definition in this way, rather than stating it outright, is so that you can understand that creativity is not a simple process and can start to think about how the issues might impinge upon your subject specialism.

REFLECTIVE TASK
REFLECTIVE TASK

Think about a lesson you have taught recently. What sort of learning was going on? Was it:

- individual?
- collaborative?
- active (involved 'doing')?
- passive (did not involve 'doing')?

How you answered this question will depend a lot on what you and your pupils were doing and on what sort of learning was taking place at the time. The fact that creativity is not a unitary construct means that we need to 'unpick' the issues associated with its teaching and learning as they appear across the secondary-school curriculum.

Creativity and learning

Just as we know that the notion of creativity is problematic, the ways people learn are also not straightforward. There is no straightforward link between teaching and learning, but we do know that the ways in which people learn are complex, and you will be forming your own views based on learning theory and on approaches to your own subject.

There is no single view of learning into which creativity slots nicely, just as there is no single view of learning which is universally applicable. As an overview and to link learning with creativity – a topic we shall return to – theories of learning can be classified under three main headings:

- *Behaviourist*: learning is a result of changes in behaviour, which occur as a result of stimulus-response mechanisms in individuals (key figures: Skinner, Thorndike).
- *Cognitive*: learning is a mental process that takes place in individuals (key figures: Piaget, Bruner).
- *Situated*: learning occurs as a result of interactions with others within a social context (key figures: Lave and Wenger, Salomon).

Some of these views are more readily associated with some subject domains than others, thus behaviourist views can be readily found in PE, cognitive views in MFL, situated views in drama. This does not mean that these are exclusive – far from it – but that your subject area may have a historical bias is favour of one of these areas.

Behaviourism

From a creativity perspective, behaviourism offers the least leeway for considerations of the role of the individual in the creative process. In this view creativity is seen as an effect, and the role of the creative person is simply that of a facilitator, a vessel in which a number of ingredients are mixed together. Skinner (1972) likened the process of writing a poem (although he said the same definition was true for art and music too) to the contribution a mother makes to her baby:

> When we say that a woman 'bears' a child, we suggest little by way of creative achievement. The verb refers to carrying the foetus to term ... But what is the nature of her contribution? She is not responsible for the skin colour, eye colour, strength, size, intelligence, talents, or any other features of her baby. She gave it half its genes, but she got those from her parents ... But she made no positive

contribution ... *The poet is also a locus, a place in which certain genetic and environmental causes come together to have a common effect. Unlike a mother, the poet has access to his poem during gestation. He may tinker with it. A poem seldom makes its appearance in a completed form. Bits and pieces* occur *to the poet, who rejects them or allows them to stand, and who puts them together to compose a poem. But they come from his past history, verbal and otherwise, and he has to learn how to put them together. The act of composition is no more an act of creation than 'having' the bits and pieces composed.*
(Skinner, 1972, pp350–5: emphasis in original)

Skinner also likened the poet in another birth-related metaphor to that of a chicken laying an egg. Mental capacity is not really involved:

We should not think of the poet as a mindful, active striving organism with all that mentalistic paraphernalia that good behaviourists do without, but rather as a locus of causation, where the contingencies of reinforcement conspire to bring a poem about. (Perkins, 1988, p382)

Behaviourism is *a dramatic shift away from psychology as the science of mental life and toward being the science of overt action* (Wasserman, 1999, p77). In the behaviourist approach, that which goes on inside people's heads is ignored and instead actions and responses are investigated. Essentially the environment is seen as a massive collection of stimuli to which the individual builds up a complicated series of responses. A behaviour can therefore be viewed as a response to a stimulus.

Creativity from a cognitive perspective

More fruitful for creativity considerations are cognitive and situated approaches. Cognitive viewpoints acknowledge that the mind is fully involved:

... generative cognitive processes are commonplace and normative. They are part of the normative operating characteristics of ordinary minds. Further, because the novel outcomes produced by these generative processes serve important processes, they satisfy the twin criteria of creative products: novelty and originality...these processes also underlie creativity in all its forms, from the most prosaic to the most exalted, from the young child who refers to cold symptoms as a 'soggy nose' to the development of the theory of relativity...
(Ward et al., 1999, p190)

This cognitivist approach allows not only for creativity to be a normal part of the mental operation of individuals, but also for Boden's notion of P- and H-creativity to have a place.

Situated views of learning place what Lave and Wenger (1991) refer to as *communities of practice* at the heart of the learning process. Learners move from novice to expert as they participate in:

.... mastery of knowledge and skill [that] requires newcomers to move toward full participation in the sociocultural practices of a community.
(Lave and Wenger, 1991, p29)

This view also places learning *in* doing, which derives from the writings of Dewey (1916), and has similarities with the work of Ryle (1949) who suggested that there are different types of knowledge, 'knowing that' and 'knowing how'.

Constructivism

One influential cognitive theory is *constructivism*. Constructivism views learning as an active process, in which the individual constructs meaning for themselves. Closely linked with this is *social constructivism*, which says that learning does not occur 'in the head' of individual pupils, but that meanings are constructed through interaction with others. This has obvious similarities with situated views of learning. The implications of social constructivism are that children can and should work in groups, in order to maximise their achievements. This has connections with Vygotsky's notion of the 'zone of proximal development' (Vygotsky, 1978), in which it is stated that there is a gap between that which pupils can do alone and that which they can do working with a more knowledgeable other.

Although there is no axiomatic link inherent between constructivist views and creativity, nonetheless the fact that pupils are making their own meanings from experiences can be seen to have a significant degree of importance, indeed Craft makes a very close connection between them:

> In a constructivist frame, learning and creativity are close, if not identical.
> (Craft, 2005b, p61)

Social constructivism and situated learning take us into the area of group work. In creativity research it is worthwhile to note that creativity is not the sole province of the individual:

> ... creativity researchers now believe that creativity cannot always be defined as a property of individuals; creativity can also be a property of groups. For example, the performance that is generated by an improvisational theatre ensemble is the creative product of the entire ensemble; there is no way to attribute the performance to any single member of the group. (Sawyer, 2003, p25)

REFLECTIVE TASK

Are there aspects of your specialist subject where group work would lend itself to creative tasks? If so, what are they? Have you used them? Have you seen teachers in school using them?

The area of group creativity is one we shall return to when we look at how teaching and learning for creativity can be organised in your classroom practice.

The place of the domain

The role of the group in creativity is not the only way in which social influences on the creative process can be seen. Csikszentmihalyi (1996) argued that for creativity to occur, even in an individual, there had to be an interplay between the individual, the domain and the field. The domain he saw as a:

> ... set of symbolic rules and procedures. Mathematics is a domain.
> (Csikszentmihalyi, 1996, p26)

The field he defined as:

> ... *all the individuals who act as gatekeepers to the domain. It is their job to decide whether a new idea or product should be included in the domain.*
> (Csikszentmihalyi, 1996, p28)

The interaction between individual, field and domain produces creativity:

> *For creativity to occur, a set of rules and practices must be transmitted from the domain to the individual. The individual must then produce a novel variation in the content of the domain. The variation then must be selected by the field for inclusion in the domain.* (Csikszentmihalyi, 1999, p315)

REFLECTIVE TASK

What are the domains and the fields in which you are working?

How are these delineated?

Who decides?

How does creativity affect your domain?

How did you define your domain? Did you say, for example, 'science' or biology? 'Art and design' or 'painting'? 'English' or 'poetry'? How you see your domain may be as a subdivision within a larger picture. Pupils may tend to view you by what it says on their timetables! This means that often you will be seen by your pupils as a representative of the *field*. It will be your judgements which determine whether a piece of work is accepted into the *domain* of your classroom. This places a lot of responsibility upon your judgements, and the formative assessments you make will be an important part of this (as we shall discuss in Chapter 5)!

Domain-specific responses

If we think about the notion of a domain and look back to Figure 1.1, then in that diagram another area of concern can be seen as being important in our investigation – that of appropriateness of response. In Figure 1.1 the endpoint is shown as arriving in a non-linear fashion from the origin; however, it is an appropriate point at which to arrive. This means that the response, although novel, is the still the sort of response which it is appropriate to produce. In other words, if you were setting up a science experiment with your pupils, gave them a box of apparatus and asked them to work out what to do with it, you would not expect a group of pupils to come back to you and say they had written a poem! A poem may be a good and creative response in, say, English, but is not what you as the science teacher expected. In other words this response is not *domain-specific*. As Csikszentmihalyi noted:

> *One can be a creative carpenter, cook, composer, chemist, or clergyman, because the domains of woodworking, gastronomy, music, chemistry, and religion exist and one can evaluate performance by reference to their traditions.*
> (Csikszentmihalyi, 1999, p315)

Creativity in the National Curriculum

So, how are the domains defined in the National Curriculum, and how does creativity figure in them? Of the twelve subjects whose programmes of study are delineated in the orders for the National Curriculum in England, eight specifically single out creative aspects of the subject in the *'importance of ...'* section, while the remaining four describe an aspect of the subject which require, at the very least, divergent thinking and may well be synonyms for creative thinking. In the order presented in the National Curriculum these statements read:

English
[English]...enables them [the pupils] to express themselves creatively and imaginatively... (p45)

Mathematics
Mathematics is a creative discipline. It can stimulate moments of pleasure and wonder... (p57)

Science
Scientific method is about developing and evaluating explanations through experimental evidence and modelling. This is a spur to critical and creative thought. (p102)

Design and Technology
They [the pupils] learn to think and intervene creatively to improve quality of life. The subject calls for pupils to become autonomous and creative problem solvers... (p134)

ICT
Pupils use ICT tools to find, explore, analyse exchange and present information responsibly, creatively, and with discrimination. (p143)

History
No direct mention, but it does say:
History fires pupils' curiosity about the past... (p148)

Geography
No direct mention, but it does say:
It can inspire them [the pupils] to think about their own place in the world... (p154)

Modern Foreign Languages

No direct mention, but it does say:

Through study of a foreign language... [pupils] begin to think of themselves as citizens of the world... (p162)

Art and Design

Art and Design stimulates creativity and imagination. (p166)

Music

[Music]... increases self-discipline and creativity, aesthetic sensitivity and fulfilment. (p171)

Physical Education

Physical Education provides opportunities for pupils to be creative... (p174)

Citizenship

No direct mention, but it does say:

It helps them [the pupils] become more informed, thoughtful and responsible... [-and it]... develops pupils' ability to reflect on issues ... (p183)

All of these statements show that there is an intention and an expectation that creativity lies at the heart of the National Curriculum. The QCA says this in an uncompromising statement:

Creative thinking and behaviour can be promoted in all national curriculum subjects and in religious education. (QCA, 2004, p9)

It will be up to you how you interpret this so as to deal with it in your domain, and to help you with this we shall be looking at specific examples as we work through this book.

Contexts for creativity

At the start of this chapter we asked 'What is creativity?' Csikszentmihalyi (1996) asked the question in a different fashion – 'Where is creativity?' The orders for the National Curriculum outlined above begin to answer this question from a legislative perspective. Other aspects of creativity and legislation in education have come in what Craft (2005a) refers to as 'three waves':

- *The first wave – the 1960s* – The Plowden Report (1967) and its aftermath, which while affecting primary schools, also impacted upon lower secondary education (what we now call KS3) too.
- *The second wave – the late 1990s*:
  - the NACCCE report (NACCCE, 1999) – this placed creativity within a cultural context similar to the *situated* perspective we discussed above;
  - the National Curriculum – whose description of creativity in *domains* we have also discussed;
  - other initiatives and publications – including *Excellence in cities* and *Improving city schools: How the arts can help* (OFSTED, 2003);
  - the role of Creative Partnerships, fostered by the Arts Council and the Department for Culture, Media and Sport;
  - the National College for School Leadership introduced a strand for fostering creativity in pupils;
  - the QCA's *Creativity: find it, promote it!* (2004) provided materials designed to promote creativity in schools.

- *The third wave – following on from the second –* characterised by notions of everyday creativity in everybody.

(After Craft, 2005a, pp8–16)

Three key classifications

The NACCCE report (NACCCE, 1999) was very influential in promoting a positive view of creativity in schools and helped codify some of the terminologies we now use on a daily basis. When discussing teaching and learning associated with creativity, there are three phrases that describe what is going on.

- **teaching creatively;**
- **teaching for creativity;**
- **creative learning.**

The first two phrases derive from the NACCCE report. The first, teaching creatively,

> *...involves teachers using imaginative approaches to make learning more interesting, exciting and effective.* (NACCCE, 1999, p6)

On the other hand, teaching for creativity entails:

> *... teachers developing young people's own creative thinking or behaviour, and includes teaching creatively.* (NACCCE, 1999, p6)

Creative learning was not defined by the NACCCE report and is not subject to definitive or universal understanding. Indeed, the very notion of there being a specific type of learning which is different from other types may strike you as odd; after all, all learning should create new meanings for the individual concerned. What distinguishes creative learning, however defined, is that it is very much an active process, where the learner is engaged in and with a task, and where this engagement results in new knowledge being formed for that individual. This is similar to the definition proposed by Jeffrey (2005):

> *The* creative *in 'creative learning' means being innovative, experimental and inventive, but the* learning *means that young participants engage in aspects of knowledge enquiry.* (Jeffrey, 2005, p37)

These three headings are key to our discussions of creativity and form the headings for the next three chapters in our discussion.

So, what do we now know about creativity, and are we now able to more definitively understand what it is? We have discussed a number of facets of creativity and decided that it is not a unitary construct. Maybe you concur with the view that:

> *Meanwhile it remains a moot point whether creativity is anything at all. Perhaps it would be better to open with 'creativities are...' and recognise straight away the potential multiplicities of what is only a notionally singular term.* (Pope, 2005, p52)

We shall refer throughout this book to creativity, but it is important to recognise that this is a device to save us continually discussing the problematic nature of the terminology. It will involve processes and products, groups and individuals, classrooms, teachers and pupils, and it will be everyday creativity with which we are likely to be concerned the most.

Looking forward: structure of this book

Throughout this book we will presenting you with a lot of information and things to try out. To help you navigate your way through this we have divided the content into three sections. The first four chapters set the scene and deal with a number of important issues. The overall plan for this part of the book is shown in Figure 1.3. Following this, Chapters 5 to 8 deal with various aspects of pedagogy and practice. The plan for this section is as shown in Figure 1.4. In Chapter 9 we consider what you will be doing in your future development and consider ways you can take the teaching and learning of creativity forwards. The plan for this final section is represented in Figure 1.5.

As we progress through the book, each chapter will extract from these diagrams the parts which are addressed, and which are taken apart and discussed in detail. Presenting the information to you in this fashion allows you to see how the overall plan of the book fits together, as well as enabling you to navigate your way round the various sections. It will also be of use to you in planning your own professional development and in auditing where your strengths lie.

A SUMMARY OF **KEY POINTS**

> **Descriptions of creativity are problematic, but notions of novelty are involved.**

> **Creativity is an active process – it involves pupils.**

> **Creativity does not solely occur in individuals – it is just as likely to be found in groups.**

> **Views of learning that involve mental processes are more likely to include creativity as a process.**

> **Creativity is specifically mentioned in the National Curriculum.**

> **There have been official initiatives to promote creativity in schools.**

FURTHER READING   FURTHER READING   **FURTHER READING**   FURTHER READING

Boden, M.A. (1990) *The creative mind: myths and mechanisms*. London: Weidenfeld Nicolson.

Craft, A. (2005) *Creativity in schools – tensions and dilemma*. Abingdon: Routledge.

Craft, A., Jeffrey, B. and Leibling, M. (eds) (2001) *Creativity in education*. London: Continuum.

Useful website

www.ncaction.org.uk/creativity/

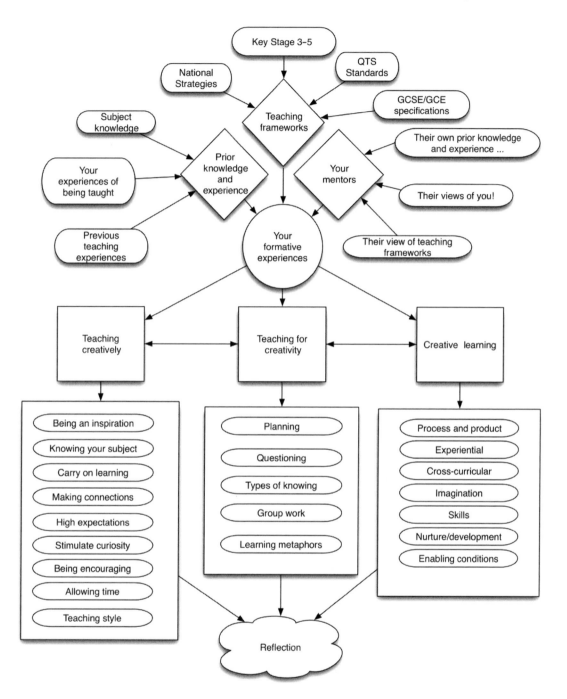

Fig. 1.3. Chapters 1–4: plan

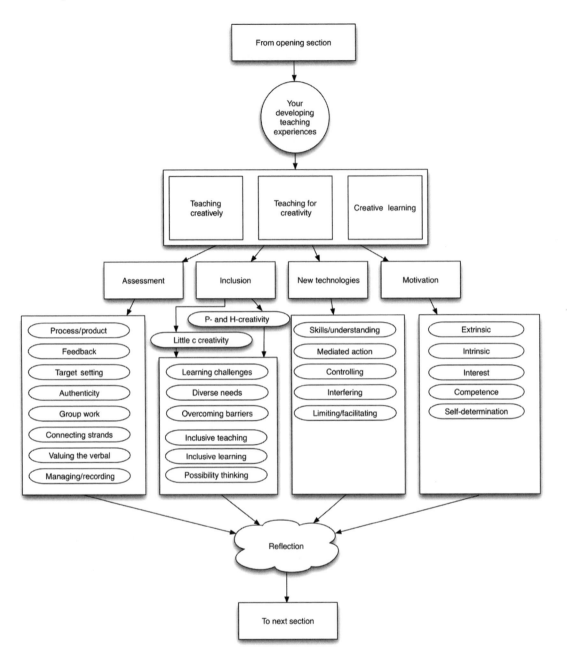

Fig. 1.4. Chapters 5–8: plan

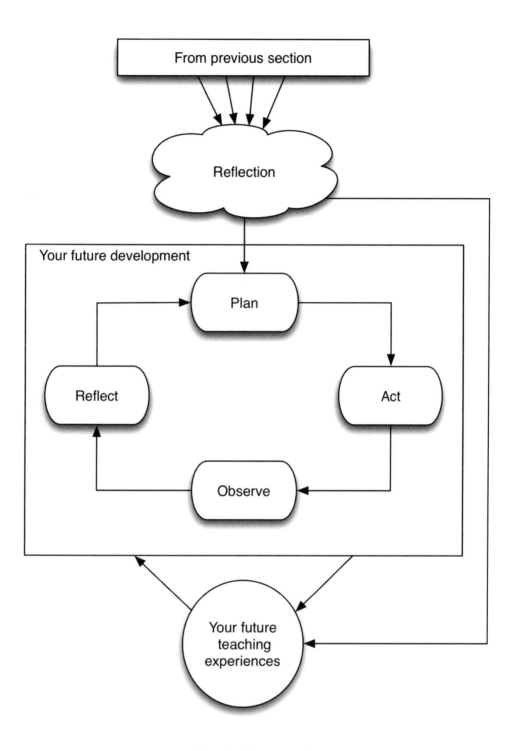

Fig. 1.5. Chapter 9: plan

REFERENCES REFERENCES **REFERENCES** REFERENCES **REFERENCES** REFERENCES

Craft, A. (2000) *Creativity across the primary curriculum: framing and developing practice*. London: Routledge.

Craft, A. (2005a) Changes in the landscape for creativity in education. In Wilson, A. (ed), *Creativity in primary education*. Exeter: Learning Matters.

Craft, A. (2005b) *Creativity in schools – tensions and dilemmas*. Abingdon: Routledge.

Csikszentmihalyi, M. (1996) *Creativity: flow and the psychology of discovery and invention*. New York: HarperCollins.

Csikszentmihalyi, M. (1999) Implications of a systems perspective for the study of creativity. In Sternberg, R.J. (ed), *Handbook of creativity*. Cambridge: Cambridge University Press, pp313–35.

de Bono, E. (1986 [1985]) *Six thinking hats*. Harmondsworth: Viking.

Dewey, J. (1916) *Democracy and education*. New York: Free Press.

Fautley, M. (2005) *CLASS: Creative learning and specialist subjects. An evaluation of Phase 1: 2004–5*. Birmingham, UK, University of Central England.

Guilford, J.P. (1967) *The nature of human intelligence*. New York: McGraw-Hill.

Jeffrey, B. (2005) *Final report of the Creative Learning and Students' Perspectives Research Project (CLASP)*. Online at: **http://clasp.open.ac.uk/project.cfm** (accessed September 2006).

Lave, J. and Wenger, E. (1991) *Situated learning: legitimate peripheral participation*. Cambridge: Cambridge University Press.

NACCCE (National Advisory Committee on Creative and Cultural Education) (1999) *All our futures: creativity, culture and education*. Sudbury, Suffolk: DfEE.

OFSTED (2003) *Improving city schools: how the Arts can help*. Document HMI 1709. London: OFSTED.

Perkins, D. (1988) The possibility of invention. In Sternberg, R. (ed), *The nature of creativity*. Cambridge: Cambridge University Press.

Plowden Report (1967) *Children and their primary schools. A report of the Central Advisory Council for Education, England*. Central Advisory Council for Education.

Pope, R. (2005) *Creativity: theory, history, practice*. London: Routledge.

QCA (1999) *The National Curriculum: handbook for secondary teachers in England; Key stages 3 and 4*. London: QCA.

QCA (2004) *Creativity: find it, promote it!* London: QCA.

Ryle, G. (1949) *The concept of mind*. Harmondsworth: Penguin Books.

Sawyer, R.K. (2003) *Group creativity: music, theater, collaboration*. Mahwah, NJ: Lawrence Erlbaum.

Skinner, B. (1972) *Cumulative record*. Englewood Cliffs, NJ: Prentice-Hall.

Smith, G.J.W. (2005) How should creativity be defined? *Creativity Research Journal,* 17 (2 & 3), 293–5.

Vernon, P. (ed) (1970) *Creativity*. London: Penguin.

Vygotsky, L. (1978) *Mind in society*. Cambridge, MA: Harvard University Press.

Wallas, G. (1926) *The art of thought*. London: Watts.

Ward, T., Smith, S. and Finke, R. (1999) Creative cognition. In Sternberg, R. (ed), *Handbook of creativity*. Cambridge: Cambridge University Press.

Wasserman, E.A. (1999) Behaviourism. In Wilson, R. and Keil, F. (eds), *The MIT encyclopedia of the cognitive sciences*. Cambridge, MA: MIT Press.

2
Teaching creatively

Introduction

Teachers cannot develop the creative abilities of their pupils if their own creative abilities are suppressed. (NACCCE, 1999, p90)

This chapter introduces the first of three important elements for creativity in the secondary curriculum, teaching creatively. Following this chapter, we will be addressing the closely related theme of *teaching for creativity* followed by *creative learning*. While these three dimensions of creativity in education are separated into distinct chapters, it will be important to bear in mind that there are many common and symbiotic elements that draw these together in the work of an experienced teacher. We will highlight some of these links as we go along.

The starting point for this chapter is the vitally important sentence drawn from the NACCCE report quoted above. This report (NACCE, 1999) made the important distinction between *teaching creatively* and *teaching for creativity*. The definition for *teaching creatively* comes in an interesting paragraph that, for reasons that will become apparent, is quoted in full below:

There is an obvious sense in which children cannot be 'taught' creativity in the way that they can be taught the times tables. Creative processes do draw from knowledge and practical skills. It is also the case that there are various techniques to facilitate creative thinking. But this does not mean that children are taught creativity by direct instruction. We define creative teaching in two ways: first, teaching creatively, and second, teaching for creativity. Many teachers see creative teaching in terms of the first (National Foundation for Educational Research (NFER) 1998, p31). Our terms of reference imply a primary concern with the second. By teaching creatively we mean teachers using imaginative approaches to make learning more interesting, exciting and effective. Teachers can be highly creative in developing materials and approaches that fire children's interests and motivate their learning. This is a necessary part of good teaching. (NACCCE, 1999, p89)

So we define teaching creatively as in the NACCCE report, namely that:

By teaching creatively we mean teachers using imaginative approaches to make learning more interesting, exciting and effective. (NACCCE, 1999, p6)

The report goes on to focus primarily on aspects related to teaching for creativity, with teaching creatively receiving little attention. At a more fundamental level, the dichotomy that the report seems to present between these two concepts is unhelpful. As Jeffrey and Craft point out:

The former [teaching creatively] may be interpreted as being more concerned with 'effective teaching' and suggest that the latter may perhaps be interpreted as having 'learner empowerment' as its main objective. Whilst the authors used these characteristics to highlight the positive nature of both teaching creatively *and* teaching for creativity *[their emphasis], nevertheless, creeping polarisation is possible if educators take up one position or the other.* (Jeffery and Craft, 2004, p77)

We are seeking to avoid any polarisation between these two important concepts. As we will see, there are important links between teaching creatively and teaching for creativity and, while we have sought to explore these in two separate chapters, we hope to impress the interrelatedness of these themes as they apply to the work of a trainee teacher. The NACCCE report also makes this important and clearly states that there is a close relationship between the two:

Teaching for creativity involves teaching creatively. Young people's creative abilities are most likely to be developed in an atmosphere in which the teacher's creative abilities are properly engaged. To put it another way, teachers cannot develop the creative abilities of their own if their creative abilities are suppressed. (NACCCE, 1999, p90)

One of the observations within the NACCCE report was that some teachers seemed to think that teaching for creativity was solely about teaching creativity. In other words, it was all about them and what they did in the classroom and did not extend to their students in any meaningful way. This is a major error and one that has been clearly exposed in recent research. However, it is clear from the NACCCE report and subsequent research that although teaching creatively is distinct from teaching for creativity in a number of ways, there are many common elements that need to be recognised. In fact, these elements could be said to characterise good teaching regardless of whether or not it has creativity as its end goal:

Teaching with creativity and teaching for creativity include all the characteristics of good teaching. These include strong motivation, high expectations, the ability to communicate and listen and the ability to interest and to inspire. Creative teachers need expertise in their particular fields. Creative teaching in mathematics involves a command of mathematical ideas and principles; creative teaching in music involves knowledge of musical forms and possibilities. But creative teachers need more that this. They need techniques that stimulate curiosity and raise self-esteem and confidence. They must recognise when encouragement is needed and confidence threatened. They must balance structured learning with opportunities for self-direction; and the management of groups with attention to individuals. They must judge the kinds of questions appropriate to different purposes and the kinds of solutions it is appropriate to expect. (NACCCE, 1999, p95)

We will be coming back to some of the specific attributes of teaching creatively later in the chapter. To reiterate, in this chapter the focus is on you as a teacher. It would be hard to imagine a successful teacher inspiring their students towards creative processes and outcomes without some element of that creative spark being evident in their own teaching.

REFLECTIVE TASK
REFLECTIVE TASK

Would you say that you are a naturally creative person?

If so, what are the specific creative skills and processes that you could bring to your new teaching role?

If not, can you identify people you know who you would say have a creative edge to their work? What are the creative skills and processes that they have? How can you seek to adopt these in your own work?

The context for teaching creatively

Training to teach is a challenging time. You will undoubtedly face many pressures and you might legitimately ask why teaching creatively should be high up the list of your priorities at this early stage of your career. We want to suggest that teaching creatively is of vital importance to you right now! Teaching creatively can be the springboard towards many other important developments that will sustain your interest throughout your teaching career. To assist you in the process of beginning to think about teaching creatively, we have designed a simple process that illustrates the main elements of this chapter and the subsequent ones focusing on teaching for creativity and creative learners (see Figure 2.1). This process is fairly self-explanatory. Here, we will briefly examine each main stage and make some general application to the task of learning to teach creatively. Following this, we will be considering some of the main elements that you will want to develop early in your teaching career and, we hope, during the teaching practices contained within your training.

Prior knowledge and experience

You are not a blank canvas! You have come to teaching with a wide range of experiences. What you think effective teaching might be will become a strong initial influence on your own teaching practice. Similarly, what you imagine a creative teacher to be will frame your early efforts to teach creatively. Where do these initial ideas about teaching come from?

Well, perhaps most importantly you have been a student yourself and studied under a range of teachers. Which of these teachers to you remember? Why? Perhaps some of them caught your imagination from an early age and inspired you to learn about their subject in a way that has maintained your interest ever since. Maybe these teachers were teaching creatively or teaching for creativity in a particularly effective manner? Perhaps other teachers had the reverse effect, and switched you off a particular subject. We all have our particular favourites. Either way, your experiences as a student colour and shape your judgement about what makes for good teaching and will also affect, fundamentally, what you consider teaching creatively to be.

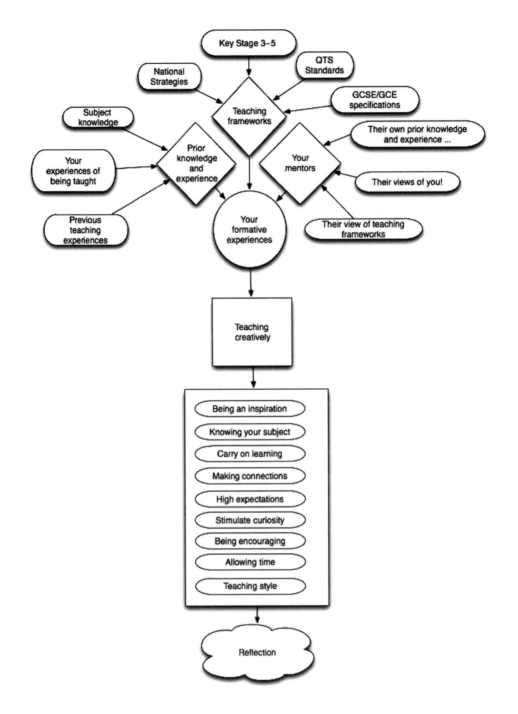

Fig. 2.1. Chapter 2: overview

Secondly, you may have done some teaching prior to embarking on an official course of study to become a qualified teacher. Perhaps you have worked in a school and watched other teachers? You might have formed opinions about their work and no doubt considered what you might have done when faced with similar classes, individual students or parents. You may also have done some teaching of your own within schools or other learning contexts. These experiences will have given you valuable insights into what effective teaching might be and caused you to think about your role as an initiator and facilitator of learning.

A third and very important part of your prior knowledge and experience is the subject knowledge that you have accumulated throughout your own education. This will vary from person to person, but you will have no doubt studied your subject to at least degree level and have developed highly specialised areas of interest within that. You will have a view on how this subject should be taught, what has worked or not for you during your undergraduate course of study and, perhaps, you will have given some thought to how it might be taught to various classes.

Auditing these three elements is an important first step for any trainee teacher. Subject knowledge audits and audits of prior teaching experiences are common elements in many initial teacher education programmes. The key point here is that when we are hypothesising about what will make you into the teacher you will want to become, there is a range of highly individual skills, knowledge, understanding and, perhaps, prejudices that you will need to challenge and consider through periods of reflection in your early teaching career. These will then help inform your work as a teacher and, importantly, influence how you seek to teach creatively.

The influence of official documentation

However, learning to teach is not just about you and what you can do. A second vital stage in your training is coming to understand, and even appreciate, the various government frameworks and initiatives that schools and teachers have to work within. These include the National Curriculum guidelines for each subject, the National Strategies, Key Stage 4 and 5 specifications and much more besides. The QTS Standards for Initial Teacher Training are another important document that will shape and influence your development as a teacher during your early training and as you move through your Induction year.

All of this official documentation influences what you think about teaching and how it should be done. You may not agree with it all. But it creates a certain expectation about how to behave, what to teach and demonstrates a range of other professional attributes. Most importantly, you will have to show, to anyone who wants to come and have a look, that you are constantly reflecting on your development (whether this be through course assessment structures during your initial training or through performance management strategies once you are working in a school).

Maybe you will consider that the bulk of official documentation that you have to deal with mitigates any real opportunity you have to teach creatively. After all, if you are constantly being told what to teach and when and how to teach it, how can you really be expected to be creative as well? This is a good question and one that many teachers are grappling with. We do not pretend to have all the answers, but we will address this point more fully below.

Your mentors

Mentors play a vital role in teacher education. Whether they are based in school, university or elsewhere, you will look to them for support, advice and guidance throughout your course of study. School-based subject mentors are recognised as being one of the most important people in a young teacher's career. Hobson noted that *student teachers consider mentoring to be a, if not the, key aspect of school-based ITT* (Hobson, 2002, p5). Your mentors will bring their own knowledge, experiences and understanding of government initiatives to bear into your own 'melting pot' of ideas about teaching.

Each of these three main areas influence your role as a teacher. You need to reflect on each area in turn and come to an awareness of your own abilities and knowledge, as well as what the government prescriptions are for teaching and learning, while keeping a good ear on the professional advice being offered to you by your mentors. But, ultimately, you have to stand in front of that group of pupils and teach them. How are you going to do it? What do you want them to learn? What are you going to say? How are you going to organise the time and resources? What questions are you going to ask? How will you know they have learnt anything? There are so many potential questions and answers may often seem lacking. But don't worry! In a short time you will get a feel for the ebb and flow of teaching your subject and many of your initial questions will be answered - and replaced by others! This is a natural part of your teacher development. All of us are still learning.

But we want to urge you, from the outset, to teach your subject in a creative way. So what does that mean?

PRACTICAL TASK PRACTICAL TASK PRACTICAL TASK PRACTICAL TASK PRACTICAL TASK

1. Spend some time auditing your previous teaching experiences and your subject knowledge. Analyse carefully the assumptions about your subject and how you think it could be taught. If possible, discuss these with others involved in initial teacher education and find out about their beliefs in this important area.

2. As you become aware of the significant pieces of government legislation surrounding teaching at Key Stages 3–5, compare the implicit assumptions within these about teaching and learning with your own views established above. Are there significant areas of agreement or division between them?

3. How receptive to advice are you? You will get lots of it during your initial teacher education programme! Devise a plan for keeping track of the advice you receive week by week from your mentors. Plan to act upon it as best you can within your own work and show a response (either through writing or your own teaching) to each issue raised. Privately, assess where your mentor's advice is 'coming from' in light of your understanding of their ideas about teaching and learning. How do these compare to your own views and understanding of government frameworks as established above?

Learning to teach creatively

We suggest that learning to teach creatively is a life-long task. But it is one that should be started early. Learning to teach creatively includes many elements, including those listed below.

- being an inspiration;
- knowing your subject inside out;
- carrying on being a learner;

- making connections: how does your subject relate to other subjects?
- developing high expectations;
- stimulating curiosity;
- being an encourager;
- balancing lessons and allowing time for students to be creative;
- finding your own teaching style.

1. Being an inspiration

Everyone remembers their good teachers, the ones that inspired them to love a particular subject or the ones that motivated and encouraged them when learning was difficult. What is it about these teachers that make them stick in your mind, even many years after you have left their classes?

Also, perhaps unfortunately, everyone remembers those teachers that didn't inspire, motivate or encourage them! For me, physics was one of those subjects I just didn't understand while at school. Imagine my surprise recently when, while working on an art and science project, I met an astrophysicist called Tim. He works at Jodrell Bank Radio Telescope (part of the University of Manchester) in Cheshire. He inspired me about space, in particular how planets and stars are born, how solar winds blow across the solar system and, of course, the sheer scale of the whole thing. On a recent visit, Tim informed me he had discovered a new star and that he was going to get the chance to name it! I enquired as to the whereabouts of this star.

If the earth were here*

and the sun were here*,

then whereabouts was his star? Approximately 3,000 kilometres away in that ↓ direction!

Now that got my attention! I wish that Tim had been my physics teacher at school. He has a way of presenting the complicated facts of astrophysics in a way that even I can understand and get excited about.

So, the first important point in this section is that we, as 'experts' in our curriculum fields, need to present the knowledge of that field in a way that inspires our students.

2. Knowing your subject inside out

In order to be an inspiration to your students, you must be completely familiar with your own subject area. This will allow you to concentrate fully on the delivery of that knowledge within the classroom. This is as true for teaching at Key Stage 3 as it is for teaching at Key Stage 5. Regardless of curriculum frameworks and modes of delivery that you will be required to work within, the students' initial source of inspiration and knowledge is you. If you are inspiring then your students will be inspired; if you are knowledgeable and can impart that knowledge in an inspirational way they will be encouraged to learn. But as we will go on to see in Chapter 3, while just knowing about your subject is vital, creating opportunities for pupils to be actively involved in the knowledge associated with your subject is equally important. This will involve you in planning carefully and setting appropriate learning objectives that allow for and facilitate opportunities for pupils to be creative learners.

3. Carrying on being a learner

Of course, all of our subjects are in a constant state of change. We never know it all. To teach creatively, it will be important for you to maintain an active interest in your subject area and the current issues and concerns that are being raised within it.

As an example, the QCA's recent consultation (*Futures – meeting the challenge*) has many interesting points of departure and application for teachers. Not least, is the challenge to explore and utilise the potential of new technologies to link subject areas within the curriculum in new ways:

> *In a technology-rich world we need to review and modernise what and how we learn. Imagine how a graphic designer works today compared with 30 years ago. What should a modernised music, art or design curriculum be like? They may use technology as a tool for thinking, making or doing. Technology needs to be used more effectively to help develop learners' enquiry skills, logical reasoning, analytical thinking and creativity. It should support individualised and independent learning, while encouraging wider communication and collaborative learning.*
> (QCA, 2005)

The QCA promotes the use of technology as a *force for change* in developing a curriculum fit for the twenty-first century. It is clear from recent QCA statements that such 'joined-up curriculum thinking' should be a priority as teachers not only seek to develop teaching skills but also the more general development of students' creativity, thinking skills, ability to communicate and ability to collaborate. We will return to this work in Chapter 5 when we consider how ICT can help us teach creatively and teach for creativity.

4. Making connections: how does your subject relate to other subjects?

While it is vital that you are able to make constructive links within your own subject area it is imperative that these also extend beyond to other related subjects. Creativity in one subject area does not exist in isolation from creativity in other subject areas. Perhaps this is a strength of much educational practice in the primary sector, where teachers have a little more flexibility to move around and between subject areas? Working within secondary education, the danger is to isolate your own subject from other related, or even non-related, disciplines in such a way that any potential creative spark that students bring with them to your lessons gets extinguished pretty quickly.

You may not feel as comfortable allowing students to develop their knowledge of other subjects within your own lessons. You may also be put under significant pressure to cover so much curriculum content the only practical consequence is that you will think that there is not any time within your lessons to allow for this kind of 'diversion'. Both of these concerns may be legitimate, but try and resist this kind of pressure. Teaching creativity must acknowledge that creativity itself is not limited to specific subject domains. In learning to teach creatively you will have to make connections across the curriculum in such a way that empowers you as a teacher to teach your subject in a new way, perhaps even in ways that you were not taught yourself! Incidentally, this will also create a more inclusive curriculum and educational environment for students, as we will consider in Chapter 6.

5. Developing high expectations

How often do you hear people moaning about today's young people? On occasions it is all too easy to disparage one's own students and put them down in front of other teachers. Try and avoid this at all costs. You have a tremendous opportunity and privilege. An important part of teaching creatively is having a high expectation of your pupils, both individual and collectively.

Spend some time getting inspired about what your pupils might be able to achieve. As a first step, why don't you visit the Creative Partnerships website and read some of the stories of other teachers and students who have worked on a range of different projects (**www.creative-partnerships.com**) in all curriculum areas. These stories can be a constant source of encouragement and a real inspiration to us as teachers about what young people can achieve given creative teaching and opportunities for developing their own creativity.

6. Stimulating curiosity

Stimulating curiosity is a vital part of teaching creatively. What is it that is particularly interesting about your subject? What might capture a Year 7 student's imagination? Are there any peculiarities or distinctive elements that you could use to engage them early on in their studies with you? Capturing and maintaining a student's interest is a prerequisite for effective teaching and learning. We believe that the majority of children are naturally curious about new things and you should seek to build on this in your teaching.

Additionally, do not fall into the trap of thinking that the only learning a student will do within your subject is within your classroom sessions. As teachers, we are constantly amazed at how students take ideas from our lessons and work through them in their own time, maybe individually or with groups of friends. The increasing availability of high-quality educational materials on the internet has revolutionised how children learn independently. Make links in your lessons to materials online that they will be able to follow up. Get away from issuing only written homework (that you will have to mark!), and encompass a broader range of resources to stimulate your students' curiosity for your subject.

7. Being an encourager

The best teachers are encouragers. There is a direct link here to teaching for creativity. Make sure that through teaching creatively you empower pupils by building them up rather than knocking them down. Communicate a 'can do' attitude in your subject rather than a 'this is difficult or complicated' one. As we will discuss in detail in Chapter 6, Craft's notion of *little c creativity* (Craft, Jeffrey and Leibling, 2001, p56) is built around the notion of *possibility thinking* as a way of life (note that this is not 'impossibility thinking'). We should apply this and state that teaching creatively is built around the notion of celebrating students' positive creative achievements.

8. Balancing lessons and allowing time for students to be creative

All teachers would like more time to teach their subject. Learning to make best use of the time that you have is an important element of teaching. Within your lessons you should seek to include a broad range of activities and opportunities for pupils to work together towards creative outcomes. Students will need the chance to work independently and learn the skills of working in a group with a range of roles. The creative processes that occur during your lessons will be facilitated by this process which we will explore in more detail in following chapters.

9. Finding your own teaching style

Finally, teaching in this way is a highly individual activity. There are many pressures on you as a trainee teacher and you may well feel that you are being told to teach in a particular way. You may even disagree on the advice you are being given! Teacher training is a process of assimilating advice, experimenting with new approaches to teaching and then evaluating the outcomes. The point here is that there is a real danger of you teaching your subject in the way that you were taught. This could be good or bad (or somewhere in between), but either way it is not based on you! Teaching creatively requires you to teach your subject as you – not as some reconstructed memory figure.

There are significant pieces of educational research that explore this issue of teacher identity (Coldron and Smith, 1999; Hargreaves, 1994; Maclure, 1993; Stronach et al., 2002). There is not the time or space to explore these in any detail here. Rather, we will leave this section with the follow advice. You may well be the only geographer, artist, musician, mathematician, etc. that your pupils will have direct access to week by week. What a tremendous privilege it is to have a group of young people looking to you for challenges, inspiration and motivation.

PRACTICAL TASK PRACTICAL TASK **PRACTICAL TASK** PRACTICAL TASK **PRACTICAL TASK**
Learning to teach creatively is a process. We have identified nine features above that could form the starting point of a plan to initiate this process in your own teaching. Using Table 2.1, set some personal targets for your own teaching drawing on these ideas.

Table 2.1 Personal targets for teaching creatively

Teaching creatively	Target	Date	Review 1 (revise target if necessary)	Date	Review 2 (revise target if necessary)	Date
Being an inspiration						
Knowing your subject inside out						
Carrying on being a learner						
Making connections: how does your subject relate to other subjects?						
Developing high expectations						
Stimulating curiosity						
Being an encourager						
Balancing lessons and allowing time for pupils to be creative						
Finding your own teaching style						

You might want to focus on a few areas to start with rather than get bogged down in too many things at once. But revisit your targets regularly and make notes about your progress. Try to create a picture of your engagement with the teaching creatively process that you can look back on at the end of your period of initial teacher education and note the positive steps that you have taken.

Conclusion

Jo Salter was the first female jet pilot in Britain. Her account of learning to fly is fascinating reading and illustrates the variety of teaching and learning methods required to become a top pilot. Of particular interest was her account of how you can learn to fly without actually being airborne:

> *I used to walk around, rehearsing the checks, the switch positions, the radio calls – running circuits in my bedroom, plotting air defence tactics across a field, circling dogfights on bikes, even flying formation in my sleep. Rehearsal builds muscles in the brain and the brain remembers this much more effectively when flying and operating an aircraft. It is the beginning of an automated sequence where pilots react without thinking – essential for rapid decision-making at life-threatening moments.* (Salter, 2005)

When Jo began to train as a teacher, she began to relate this process of learning to the challenges associated with teaching:

> *As a teacher I employ the same lessons that I learnt as a student; I rehearse and visualise – how I am going to stand and how I am going to use my body language in order to convey my message. The spoken word is only part of how we teach. We have all experienced the flat teacher, the one who seems to no longer be there, whose energy has disappeared and whose presence is blurred. These are not the lessons you remember.* (Salter, 2005)

Pre-lesson rehearsals are a vital part of turning a lesson plan into a reality. Reading through, acting out or practising certain key parts of a lesson plan will be of benefit for all teachers as they seek to develop new strategies for learning to teach creatively. Structure explanatory dialogue or key questions and, if necessary, mentally script parts of the lesson plan ensuring that there is clarity and purpose in your words.

Perhaps you have found this a strange conclusion? What has it got to do with teaching creatively? We suggest that teaching creatively is not about a lack of planning and preparation and allowing things to just 'happen' in your classroom. If anything, teaching creatively requires more rigorous planning and preparation. It depends on you being completely familiar with your subject and concentrating whole-heartedly on your teaching role. It will require you to rehearse key moments and points of instruction, perhaps in the way that Salter had done. Teaching creatively can be conceptualised as an artistic, musical or dramatic performance or even a flight in a military aircraft! It is not an exact science and requires you to be highly responsive, reflective and self-aware. Your role is multifaceted and complex. You can be an initiator, responder, facilitator, critical friend, listener, co-performer, improviser and much more besides. But it is fun, engaging and rewarding! It is vital that you do not lose sight of the need for a skilful performance to be central to your teaching, particularly if you are seeking to teach creatively.

A SUMMARY OF **KEY POINTS**

> Teaching creatively and teaching for creativity are distinct but related concepts. Both of them need to be developed in your teaching if you are to become an effective teacher and if your students are going to become creative learners.

> Your teaching does not take place in a vacuum. You will need to be aware and critical of your own prior experiences of teaching and learning, the government's agenda for your subject and teaching/learning at each key stage, and the advice of other professionals.

> Teaching creatively is an ideal first step towards becoming an effective teacher. You should plan to teach creatively from the very beginning of your teaching career, i.e. during your initial school-based placements.

> Learning to teach creatively is a very personal thing, but there are common elements, skills and understandings that you can develop. Each of these must be grounded in effective and focused planning and preparation for each lesson.

REFERENCES REFERENCES **REFERENCES** REFERENCES **REFERENCES** REFERENCES

Coldron, J. and Smith, R. (1999) Active location in teachers' construction of their professional identities. *Journal of Curriculum Studies*, 31 (6), 711–26.

Craft, A., Jeffrey, B. and Leibling, M. (2001) *Creativity in education*. London and New York: Continuum.

Hargreaves, A. (1994) *Changing teachers, changing times: teacher's work and culture in the postmodern age*. London: Cassell.

Hobson, A. (2002) Student teachers' perceptions of school-based mentoring in initial teacher training. *Mentoring and Tutoring*, 10 (1), 5–20.

Jeffrey, B. and Craft, A. (2004) Teaching creatively and teaching for creativity: distinctions and relationships. *Educational Studies*, 30 (1), 77–87.

Maclure, M. (1993) Arguing for your self: identity as an organising principle in teachers' jobs and lives. *British Educational Research Journal*, 19 (4), 311–22.

NACCCE (1999) *All our futures: creativity, culture and education*. Sudbury, Suffolk: DfEE.

National Foundation for Educational Research (NFER) (1988) *CAPE UK: Stage one evaluation report*. Slough: NFER.

QCA (2005) *Futures: meeting the challenge* ('Forces for change', point 2). Online at: **www.qca.org.uk** (accessed 1 February 2005).

Salter, J. (2005) Final word. *Report*, July/August, p30. London: Association of Teachers and Lecturers.

Stronach, I., Corbin, B., McNamara, O., Stark, S. and Warne, T. (2002) Towards an uncertain politics of professionalism: teacher and nurse identities in flux. *Journal of Education Policy*, 17 (1), 109–38.

3
Teaching for creativity

By the end of this chapter you should:

- **have considered how teaching for creativity affects your role as a teacher;**
- **have considered how you can teach your subject to foster and encourage creativity;**
- **have learned about theoretical approaches to creativity and learning;**
- **have developed theories, concepts, ideas and strategies to enable you to teach for creativity.**

This chapter will help you to meet the following Professional Standards for QTS:

Q1, Q3, Q4, Q6, Q7, Q8, Q10, Q18, Q19, Q22, Q25, Q28, Q29, Q30

Introduction

This chapter investigates the main issues from the overall diagram, as shown in Figure 3.1

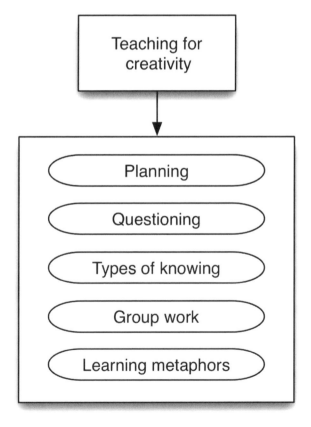

Fig. 3.1. Chapter 3: overview

Planning for creativity

Sometimes a creative moment can happen unexpectedly in your classroom. While some teachers are able to take as their mantra *the unexpected is expected in my lessons* (OFSTED, 2003, p8), for others the unexpected, while maybe not a daily occurrence, will nonetheless be most welcome. However, in teaching for creativity what you hope to do is plan for the unexpected to take place. This requires you to think about what you want to happen, and how you can best facilitate this happening. Let us also be clear on what we do not want:

> *A ... misconception is that creativity is to do with free expression. This is partly why there's such concern about creativity in education. Critics think of children running wild and knocking down the furniture: with being spontaneous and uninhibited rather than with serious academic work.* (Robinson, 2001, p113)

This is *not* what we are discussing, and key to this is the notion of *planning*. You will be planning for purposeful activity, and this will be a help. We know that planning what will take place in a lesson can be a major aspect of ensuring good on-task behaviour. We also know that *Most effective teachers anticipate and prevent disruption by careful planning ...* (Crozier, 2004, p143). You will probably have some form of planning documentation that you are required to use in the form of lesson plans, units or schemes of work, and reflections or evaluations of lessons. Working within existing structures like this will give you a good background in planning for creativity to take place.

Types of knowledge

One aspect of planning which is likely to figure in whatever documentation you use is that of *learning*. The notion of learning outcomes (or *objectives*, or *fulfilments*, or however they are referred to in your documentation) is that you plan in advance for what the pupils will *learn* in the sessions you are teaching them. Note that this is distinct from ideas of *task*, *doing* or *activity* outcomes. These two types of outcome, *learning* and *task*, have a number of commonalities with two separate types of knowledge *procedural* and *declarative*. Procedural knowledge is knowledge about how to do something and is a sort of knowledge which may not be easily communicated in words. Declarative knowledge, also called *propositional knowledge*, is a knowledge of facts, knowledge which can normally be conveyed (*declared*) in words. These two types of knowledge were also described as being 'knowing that' and 'knowing how' by Ryle (1949).

REFLECTIVE TASK

Thinking about your subject domain, consider:

- a type of knowledge which is procedural, about how to do something;
- a type of knowledge which is declarative, about facts or information.

Writing learning outcomes in advance of teaching a unit of work is not easy – it is much easier to write task outcomes, as you can legislate for what the pupils will *do* far more straightforwardly than what they will *learn*. Don't worry if this is the case for you – you are not alone:

... novice teachers have difficulty constructing objectives (both intellectually and semantically), more so if they have to be delineated before they have even considered the methods, activities, resources, or central idea of the lesson ... (John, 2006)

In order to help with your planning, let us consider the nature of learning and task outcomes, and provide some examples. Table 3.1 shows learning considered separately from doing; the column on the left shows the learning which will hopefully arise from the doing on the right.

Table 3.1 Exemplar outcomes

Learning outcomes *In this lesson I want the pupils to learn:*	**Task outcomes** *In this lesson I want the pupils to:*
How to inflate a balloon with an air-pump	Fix the balloon properly onto the pump before they begin inflation
Why William won the Battle of Hastings	Place a sequence of cards describing events in 1066 into a logical order
Whether there is a direction called 'up' when you are in space	Model planetary movements using balls in the playground
That the creative process involves planning and revisiting ideas	Hold discussions in groups of 4–5 which result in a plan on paper before they start work
The best way to mix colour paints	Use the paints to produce specified outcome

All of the items in Table 3.1 are legitimate learning outcomes and lead to logical tasks. Planning for learning in this way focuses your attention onto the heart of the matter – teaching for creativity – in that learning is at the heart of what you are doing, the pupils are *learning by doing*, a perspective that dates back to Dewey in the early years of the twentieth century.

Let us now consider the nature of the planning process you will go through in planning a lesson or series of lessons. Figure 3.2 gives a diagrammatic representation of such a planning process and gives you question headings for learning and task outcomes in order to help you through this process.

The emphasis in Figure 3.2 is on *learning* in that pupil competences in *tasks* and *skills* are used to inform the learning decisions that you will be making. Notice too the relevance of prior learning – you will need to make decisions about how to sequence your creative activities so that pupils have the necessary skills and concepts to be able to work at the creative activity you are planning. The questions in the boxes on the left-hand side of the diagram take you through a series of issues concerned with learning. The boxes on the right of the diagram *inform* your answers to these questions by focusing your attention onto task issues but again, notice that the tasks are there to help with learning.

PRACTICAL TASK PRACTICAL TASK **PRACTICAL TASK** PRACTICAL TASK **PRACTICAL TASK**

Use Figure 3.2 to design a learning activity involving creativity in your subject area for a *specific* class or group. Choose a single learning episode for this, maybe a straightforward problem such as:

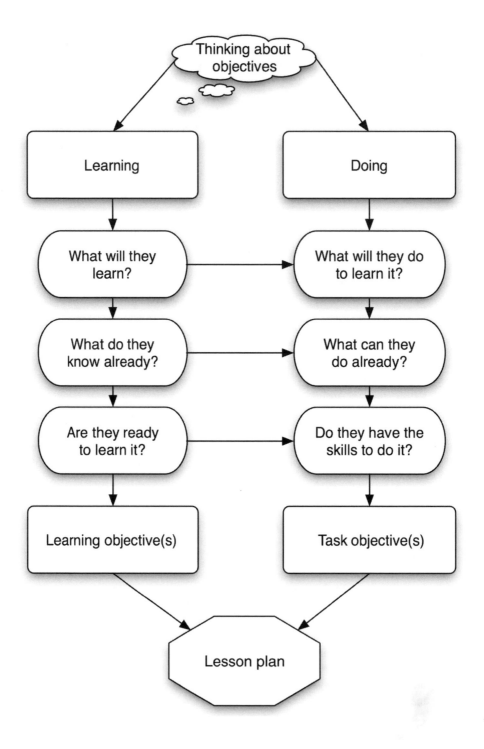

Fig. 3.2. Planning objectives

- **setting up an experiment;**
- **scoring a goal from a distance;**
- **remembering details from a map;**
- **making up a short melody;**
- **writing the first verse of a poem.**

Work through the questions in order, thinking about what your students know and can do already, and what the learning and task outcomes will be.

We will look at planning for creativity again later – Chapter 4 in particular picks up the thread, looking at the processes involved when planning for creative learning.

Questioning

In thinking about teaching for creativity, each of the learning and task outcomes in Table 3.1 describe specific types of knowledge and activity. What you want to do in your lessons is to direct the pupils towards creative processes, and in order to do this you need to think about how you will enable pupils to make progress in their learning and doing. A key component of this is questioning. Polanyi (1967, p4) wrote of how we can know more than we can tell, and with pupils this is especially likely to be the case. So, in order to try and access pupil knowledge you will need to develop questioning skills. A useful starting point for this is Bloom's taxonomy (Bloom, 1956). Bloom and his team developed a classification of levels of thinking according to cognitive complexity. They also found that at the time 95 per cent of teacher questions were at the lowest level! Bloom classified and labelled six categories of thought. Bloom's taxonomy was revised nearly 50 years later by Anderson and Krathwohl (2001). Figure 3.3 shows both the original Bloom taxonomy and the later version side by side. Both of these taxonomies are hierarchical: levels near the bottom represent lower orders of thinking, moving towards the apex which represents higher-order thinking.

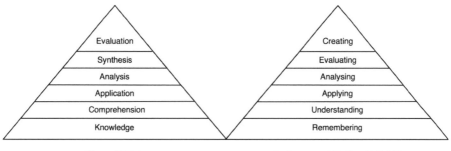

Bloom (1956)   Anderson and Krathwohl (2001)

Fig. 3.3 Bloom's taxonomy and revision

There are some significant alterations between the two versions. The Anderson and Krathwohl version changes the nouns to verbs, moves 'evaluating' down to take the place of 'synthesis' and adds a new top layer of 'creating'. For our purposes this is both helpful in that it places *creating* into a framework of ways you can direct questioning, but is also seemingly problematic in that it appears that creating is the final stage in a sequence of cognitive processes. However, this raising of *creating* to higher-order thinking does not place it out of reach: what is does is to make it a logical part of the thought processes of your pupils.

One of the tasks for you as a teacher is to develop the thinking skills of your pupils. Devise one question for each of the first three levels of the taxonomy (three questions in all) which helps check if the pupils are able to *remember, understand* and *apply* a specific concept.

Maybe you found this quite challenging? Asking questions is a skill, and like all skills, needs practice to develop. Let us think about this and give you some starting points.

We have already noted how the each of the learning and task outcome statements listed in Table 3.1 provide clues about the type of knowledge or skills involved. Let us now do the same for the various aspects of Bloom's taxonomy. Taking each of the levels of Bloom's taxonomy, let us revisit the Practical Task above and ask what sort of cognitive involvement is happening in each and what questioning for this would look like. To do this we shall use both the original Bloom taxonomy and the more recent version, as some documentation you will meet in school (*inter alia* DfES, 2002) refers to the original, while others refer to the update. Table 3.2 shows the cognitive activity involved in each aspect of the taxonomy.

Table 3.2 Cognitive activity

Taxonomy descriptor	Cognitive activity
Creating	Come up with original ideas
Evaluating	Make judgements about effectiveness
Synthesis	Use multiple understandings
Analysing	Reflecting on understanding
Applying	Use understanding
Understanding	Demonstrate they know something
Remembering	Recalling information

The broad outlines of the right-hand column of Table 3.2 delineate cognitive activity, or what the pupils will be doing, in order to demonstrate achievement at each level. These are helpful in devising question areas as they help you think about what you and the pupils should be focusing on.

One way which many trainee and beginning teachers have found helpful in devising questions to develop knowledge is to start with a list of question 'stems' which form the first part of what you will ask. Table 3.3 provides some possible stems which you can use to devise questions for each level of the taxonomy.

Table 3.3 Question stems for Bloom's taxonomy

Knowledge/	Describe ...
remembering	Describe what you are doing ...
	Show me what you are doing ...
	Can you remember how to ...
	Identify ...
	Can you recall ...

Comprehension/ *understanding*	What is the idea behind this ... Can you show me an example where you ... What differences are there ... What is going on at this point ... Can you demonstrate ... Explain ... Illustrate ...
Application/ *applying*	How will you go about ... What will you do to ... Can you think of (*or show me*) an instance where ... How will you carry out ...
Analysis/ *analysing*	How might it have been different if ... What happens in the bit when you ... Can you explain what went on as you were doing that bit where ... Compare that with ... Can you distinguish between that and ... Are you able to describe how you ...
Synthesis	What would happen if you were to put your ideas together with hers ... What would happen if you changed that bit where ... How could you do this differently ...
Evaluation/ *evaluating*	What was successful ... What changes might you make ... Can you justify ... How do you feel about ... Why do you think that ... Are you able to suggest ...
Creating	Can you come up with a solution ... Are you able to devise ... Can you generate ... How about a different response ... What would that look like ... What would that sound like ... How would that be made up ... Can you produce ...

Using the stems in Table 3.3 you should be able to formulate questions that probe students' knowledge, concepts and skills. You should also find that you are able to use these stems to advance pupil thinking, by moving them from one level to another.

REFLECTIVE TASK

How do the questions you devised in the *practical task* above compare with the questioning stems in Table 3.3?

In the revised version of Bloom's taxonomy, *creating* forms a natural conclusion to the other modes of thinking. We can use this to our advantage in that creative thinking can flow naturally from almost any topic which entails cognitive processes.

Short-circuiting Bloom

Bloom's taxonomy proposes a hierarchy which results in creativity. It can be argued that moments of everyday creativity do not need to occur at the end of this long and complex process. For example, one aspect of creativity we have not yet discussed is that of jokes! A joke often involves a creative interpretation of words or situations to come up with a new and surprising outcome, and these can be considered creative. Linking jokes into a discussion of creativity Koestler (1964) proposed that there exist patterns of human thought and behaviour – he calls these *matrices* – which are governed by sets of rules or codes. When two independent matrices interact with each other, then what happens is:

> ... either a collision ending in laughter, or their fusion in a new intellectual synthesis, or their confrontation in an aesthetic experience. (Koestler, 1964, p45)

In this way Koestler describes the way that the creative act can be accounted for in humour, in science and in the arts. He calls the results of this collision *bisociation* – linked with association, but happening in two areas simultaneously. For our purposes in the classroom this notion is helpful, as the collision of two ways of thinking can happen to anyone, at any time. Creativity can therefore be the result of a sudden flash of inspiration, as well as a steady progression through a hierarchy.

Knowledge and creativity

We have so far been considering ways of developing pupil knowledge and at the same time moving them towards a position where they are able to be creative. We looked earlier at the difference between *declarative* and *procedural* knowledge. Creative thinking operates tangentially to these. Creative moments are likely to occur once pupils have assimilated enough information to allow them to think in such a way as to make new connections, or develop new insights. As Runco (2003, p320) notes: *In Piagetian terms, assimilation is the key to creative thinking. It is there that the individual takes liberties with information.* *Assimilation* involves a level of mastery of the domain, and so knowledge, once assimilated, has the potential to be used in novel ways. From this notion of assimilation it is a short step to a consideration of that which is referred to by Craft (2000, 2001, 2005) as *possibility thinking*:

> ...possibility thinking means refusing to be stumped by circumstances, but being imaginative in order to find a way round a problem or in order to make sense of a puzzle. (Craft, 2000, p4)

Possibility thinking is therefore a process of imaginative thinking. Imagination is a cognitive activity that can be developed and fostered, and this takes us back to the use of questioning, as Craft goes on to observe that:

> ... *learning opportunities need to both stimulate and support the posing of questions by children and their teachers ...* (Craft, 2000, p6)

We looked earlier at question stems that the teacher can use to promote learning. Good modelling of these will enable pupils to do this too, and this is turn will help them to develop their own thinking as they become increasingly proficient at asking themselves and each other suitable questions. This is another recurring theme, where you as teacher *model* outcomes that you wish to reinforce. Modelling good questioning is an enabling condition which will benefit your pupils. Getting them to ask questions of each other will help consolidate their learning and allow them to cooperate effectively.

The notion of pupils developing their own learning takes us into two further areas which have a role to play in teaching for creativity; these are *metacognition* and *group learning*.

Metacognition

Metacognition refers to pupils reflecting on their own thought processes, or 'thinking about thinking', and can be defined as:

> ... *the process of planning, assessing, and monitoring one's own thinking. Thinking about thinking in order to develop understanding ...* (**www.standards.dfes.gov.uk/ thinkingskills/glossary/**)

Developing metacognition in the case of teaching for creativity involves discussing with pupils the thought processes they are going through and reflecting on how they arrived at the decisions they have made, not just on what those decisions were. We have already discussed the role of structured questioning in developing pupil thinking. The same process can be used to foster metacognition by making questioning reflexive and getting pupils to think about how they arrived at their answers. This is a development from the questioning skills discussed earlier, and again needs practice to establish it. Figure 3.4 shows an outline of the way in which you can plan for this.

The *direct questions* box in Figure 3.4 would begin with one of the questions you had planned from our discussion concerning Bloom's taxonomy earlier. This first questioning episode is intended to clarify pupil thought, not only allow them to advance through to higher-level thinking but also to provide you with insights into their responses and allow you to give feedback (see also Chapter 5). The notion of a *questioning episode* is an apposite one here: questions are likely to be sequential, and you will need to rehearse 'thinking on your feet' in order to ask a sequence of questions effectively and gauge your subsequent questioning from pupil responses you receive. Once this initial questioning episode has been completed, you are then able to move to the second questioning episode. Here your focus of attention will be on questioning to help pupils understand their own thinking. Again, this is likely to be a sequence of questions which will evolve in response to pupils' answers and comments.

The final stage is shown as the third questioning episode. This is not an essential part of the process but something that established teachers often do – where the pupils are left with something to think about that does not require an immediate response. This is useful in that it allows an extended 'wait time' (Rowe, 1974) before the pupils need to answer. Giving the pupils time to think has been shown to improve the quality of response gained during

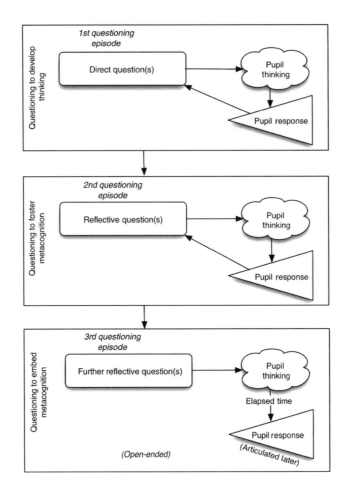

Fig. 3.4. Questioning for metacognition

questioning, so this undoubtedly will be of assistance. When working with a number of groups in a classroom simultaneously it also gives you a point of focus when you return your attention at a later stage – you can ask whether they have thought about the issues concerned.

RESEARCH SUMMARY RESEARCH SUMMARY RESEARCH SUMMARY RESEARCH SUMMARY

Wait time

Wait time occurs when teachers allow pupils time to think in response to a question, before taking *any* answers. The notion was first proposed by Mary Budd Rowe in 1974 (Rowe, 1974). She found that:

> ... teachers allow an average of one second for a response to a question, and follow a student response by a comment within an average of nine-tenths of a second. When these two 'wait times' are extended to three to five seconds, a number of changes occur in student variables. There are increases in the length of the response, the number of unsolicited appropriate responses, student confidence, incidence of speculative responses, incidence of child-child data comparisons, incidence of evidence-inference statements, frequency of student questions, and incidence of responses from 'relatively slow' students. (Rowe, 1974, abstract)

This idea has been taken up more recently in the Secondary Strategy (DfES, 2002), where it is recommended that:

> *Teachers should build in 'wait time' so that pupils can reflect on a challenging question before answering it.* (DfES, 2003, p6)

Members of the influential Assessment Reform Group (ARG) have also recommended that teachers use wait time as a useful strategy for developing and extending pupil thinking:

> *A consequence of such short 'wait time' is that the only questions that 'work' are those that can be answered quickly, without thought – that is, questions calling for memorized facts ... Increasing the wait time can help more students become involved in discussions and increase the length of their replies. Another way to broaden participation is to ask students to brainstorm ideas, perhaps in pairs, for two to three minutes before the teacher asks for contributions. Overall, a consequence of such changes is that teachers learn more about the students' prior knowledge and about any gaps and misconceptions in that knowledge, so that teachers' next moves can better address the learners' real need.* (Black et al., 2004, pp11–12)

PRACTICAL TASK PRACTICAL TASK PRACTICAL TASK PRACTICAL TASK PRACTICAL TASK

To improve the quality of answers you get in response to your questioning in class, try telling the pupils you are going to wait for, say, ten seconds before taking any answers. You might need to practise this, as a few seconds can seem much longer in the classroom!

The type of questions you ask to develop metacognition are ones which, again, it helps if you plan for in advance. Here are some sample question stems to help you with this:

Questions for metacognition:
What evidence do you have for ...?
Is that your opinion, or a fact?
Why do you think this is right?
Why are you doing it like this?
How did you decide how to label/classify that?
How did you measure that?
How do you know your measurement is accurate?
Would someone else doing this come up with the same answers/measurements/responses?
Are you able to make any generalisations?
Does this make sense to you?
How does this fit with theoretical accounts?
In this what you expected?
How would you go about explaining this to someone else?
What did you have to do to solve this problem?
What does [this] mean?
Can you give an example of where you have seen something like this elsewhere?

PRACTICAL TASK PRACTICAL TASK PRACTICAL TASK PRACTICAL TASK PRACTICAL TASK

Prepare some questions for developing pupil metacognition that you can ask next time you have the opportunity. It may seem odd planning for individual questions, but you will find that once you have done this a few times you will be able to move smoothly from one type of question to another.

Having considered the roles of metacognition in developing learning, thinking and creativity, we now turn our attention to an important aspect of fostering creativity in the classroom, that of pupils working cooperatively in groups.

Learning and creativity in groups

In Chapter 1 we introduced the notion of creativity taking place as a group activity, and we discussed how this could be linked to a constructivist view of learning. In considering how you can develop a pedagogy which fosters and embraces creativity in your classroom, we need to look into group learning and group creativity in more detail.

Theoretical issues

Theoretical stances on group learning tend to come from four principal but related domains:

- **social constructivism;**
- **activity theory;**
- **situated learning;**
- **distributed cognition.**

Social constructivism

We looked briefly at social constructivism in the opening chapter. We now discuss it in more detail. Social constructivists believe that the acquisition of knowledge takes place on a broader canvas than that of the individual mind alone. Most social constructivist views can be traced back to Vygotsky, whose view of learning:

> ... regards individual cognitive development as subject to a dialectical interplay between nature and history, biology and culture, the lone intellect and society. Vygotsky believed that mind is transmitted across history by means of successive mental sharings which pass ideas from those more able or advanced to those who are less so ... (Roth, 1999, p10)

This mixture of influences also accounts for the different names by which social constructivism can be found, as variants on it are also to be found discussed as socio-cultural or socio-historical approaches. The essential feature of Vygotsky's work in this domain is that the individual finds things out first by their interaction with others, and then they become part of the intellectual functioning of that individual:

> Every function in the child's cultural development appears twice: first, on the social level, and later, on the individual level; first, between people (interpsychological) and then inside the child (intrapsychological). This applies equally to voluntary attention, to logical memory, and to the formation of concepts. All the higher functions originate as actual relationships between individuals.
> (Vygotsky, 1978, p57)

The zone of proximal development

The point at which knowledge moves from the social level to the individual occurs in the *zone of proximal development*, which we met briefly in Chapter 1. The zone of proximal development (ZPD) is the difference between that which a child can achieve alone, and that which they can achieve with a more knowledgeable other, whether that is an adult or a peer. Figure 3.5 shows a diagrammatic representation of this.

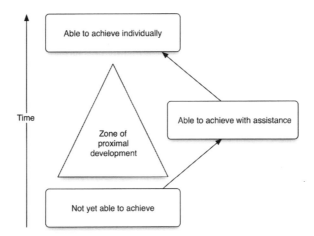

Fig. 3.5. Zone of proximal development

The meaning of working in the ZPD is that pupils are able to achieve at a higher level than they would be able to on an individual basis.

REFLECTIVE TASK

Think back to an occasion when you have seen pupils helping each other to do or understand something in a lesson you have taught or have observed. Consider how the notion of the ZPD might account for the way in which this took place.

If you cannot immediately recall such a learning episode, be on the lookout for one next time you are observing a class.

There is a caveat here though with regard to your planning: it is important that you do not think of the ZPD as being something which you need to socially engineer in order to achieve, so that pupils can work with those of a 'higher' or 'lower' ability. In fact, the very notion of *ability* is itself a problematic construct.

REFLECTIVE TASK

What do you understand if a teacher says a pupil has a high ability?

Often responses to this lie in the area of being able to speak and write to a good standard, or of being 'with-it' in a mental sense. Sometimes an element of subject-specific judgement will be made too, especially in areas where achievement is *evidenced in action*, such as dance, sports, drama, art, poetry, story writing or music.

When teachers talk of ability they are often using the term as a shorthand for the intelligence that some IQ tests measure, essentially verbal and mathematical. As Howard Gardner noted:

> ... *most testing instruments are biased heavily in favour of two varieties of intelligence – linguistic and logical-mathematical. Individuals blessed with this particular combination are likely to do well on most kinds of formal tests, even if they are not particularly adept in the domain under investigation.* (Gardner, 1999, p101)

To counter this problem, Gardner suggested that IQ testing alone is not a sufficient way to describe the achievements or potential of an individual and, instead, we should be considering that people have multiple intelligences (MI) in a number of domains. This is the origin of Gardner's MI theory (Gardner, 1983).

RESEARCH SUMMARY RESEARCH SUMMARY RESEARCH SUMMARY RESEARCH SUMMARY

Gardner's theory of multiple intelligences

Gardner's MI theory identifies a number of areas where individuals have specific abilities or intelligences. These are:

- **Verbal-linguistic intelligence** – well-developed verbal skills and sensitivity to the sounds, meanings and rhythms of words.
- **Mathematical-logical intelligence** – ability to think conceptually and abstractly, and able to discern logical or numerical patterns.
- **Musical intelligence** – ability to produce and appreciate rhythm, pitch and timbre.
- **Visual-spatial intelligence** – capacity to think in images and pictures, to visualise accurately and abstractly.
- **Bodily-kinesthetic intelligence** – ability to control one's body movements and to handle objects skilfully.
- **Interpersonal intelligence** – capacity to detect and respond appropriately to the moods, motivations and feelings of others.
- **Intrapersonal intelligence** –capacity to be self-aware and in tune with own inner feelings, values, beliefs and thinking processes.
- **Naturalist intelligence** – ability to recognise and categorise plants, animals and other objects in nature.
- **Existential intelligence** – sensitivity and capacity to tackle deep questions about human existence, such as the meaning of life, why do we die and how did we get here.

In a consideration of the various ways in which you might place pupils into a group, employment of Gardner's theory would imply that, however you establish combinations of individuals into groups, they will not have a homogenous selection of abilities, and that therefore all groupings in the classroom will contain pupils with differing abilities. For group learning situations in the classroom this in itself is not problematic, as in a group:

> ... *each participant makes significant contributions to the emergent understandings of all members, despite having unequal knowledge concerning the topic under study ...* (Palincsar et al., 1993, p43)

What this means for you as a teacher is that all pupils will be able to work, with differing levels of ability, with each other. What you should be doing is to make choices based on your assessment of *the abilities that matter* in the context within which you wish the pupils to work.

REFLECTIVE TASK

What abilities matter in your subject area?

Do you know to what extent the pupils possess these – if so, how?

Activity theory

Vygotsky's notion of the ZPD is one of *activity*, in that achievements which are taking place are occurring *between* individuals. The importance of activity in this way of looking at things takes us to the next theoretical area we shall be considering, that of *activity theory*.

Activity theory (AT) concerns itself with the:

> ... *psychological impacts of organised activity and the social conditions and systems which are produced in and through such activity.* (Daniels, 2001, p84)

One of the items of activity which AT introduces is the notion of *mediating artefacts*, which can be considered both as 'real' tools, such as computers, paint and writing, and as mental constructs, such as speaking, gesture and expressions. These mediating artefacts act *between* the individual and the outcome, sometimes in obvious ways, as in a drawing accomplished with a brush, sometimes in less obvious ways, such as an idea which arises jointly out of discussion. This intertwining relationship is usually represented graphically in the form of a triangle as in Figure 3.6.

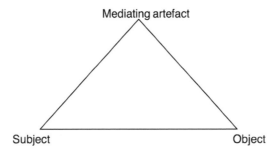

Mediating artefact

Subject   Object

Fig. 3.6. Activity theory triangle (after Cole and Engestrom (1993) and Daniels (2001))

In Figure 3.6 *subject* refers to an individual, *object* to the outcome of the activity, and *mediating artefact* to the thing used by the individual to arrive at the outcome.

This notion of mediating artefacts is a useful one for us in our thinking about creativity, as the resources – the equipment and apparatus – used for a creative activity will have a direct influence not only on the type of activity that is undertaken, but also on the products that result from the activity. This is an important notion, particularly with regard to the use of ICT, and is looked at again in Chapter 6.

REFLECTIVE TASK

Can you name some *mediating artefacts* for your subject area?

Are these real, tangible objects, or thoughts and concepts?

How are they used?

Situated learning and distributed cognition

When undertaking an activity in the ZPD, learners need others. As they become increasingly proficient they are able to operate autonomously. This takes us to Lave and Wenger's (1991) work on *situated learning* and especially on *legitimate peripheral participation.* This means participants in group learning situations move along a continuum from being novices towards becoming more expert. What happens, in this view, is that knowledge is *distributed* among and between groups of people.

Working in a group means that not only can physical tasks be distributed among members of a group but that cognitive tasks can too. This allows for pupils to work on separate aspects of the creative process, but work on them together. In this sense it is the case that the whole is greater than the sum of the parts. Figure 3.7 presents a graphical representation of this process, where the circles represent five members of a group and the pentagon represents the creative process *distributed* among them. No one pupil has ownership of the process, and the process exists *between* them.

The notions of situated learning and distributed cognition are linked, as Salomon (1993, p 114) notes:

> ... *if cognitions are distributed, then by necessity they are also situated ...*

In other words, learning is involved in both *doing* and *participating*.

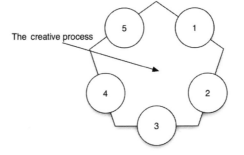

Fig. 3.7. Distributed creativity

Implications for the classroom

Sometimes it seems teachers use group activities in the classroom as pragmatic substitutes for individual work. The theoretical approaches we have been discussing here are not like this at all because they emphasise that group activity is not only an appropriate process in its own right, but that it is effective and desirable as a way of working. Indeed (Sawyer, 2003) notes that:

> ... *group creativity is rather common and accessible; in contrast to creativity in privileged domains such as the arts and sciences, all humans have some ability to participate creatively in groups.* (Sawyer, 2003, p122)

REFLECTIVE TASK

REFLECTIVE TASK

Think about the last time you saw some group work in a classroom.

Why was group work used?

Was anything achieved that could not have been achieved with pupils working individually? If so, what?

Group constitution

Having given some thought as to theoretical positions on group creativity, we now turn to more practical matters and consider how you can establish groups in your lessons and what the make-up of such groups might be.

Useful guidance for this is given in the *Literacy across the curriculum* strand of the KS3/ Secondary Strategy (DfES, 2001). Here groupings are classified according to size and type. Size groupings are as listed below:

- individual;
- pair;
- small group 3–4;
- large group 6–7;
- whole class.

As you plan for the creative activity you will be thinking about which of these ways of organising pupils will be most appropriate for you.

REFLECTIVE TASK

REFLECTIVE TASK

When you have seen group work taking place, which of the size groups did you observe?

Are there any size groupings you have *not* seen? Why might that be?

Types of groupings are as listed below.

- friendship groups;
- ability groups;
- structured mix;
- random mix;
- single sex.

Friendship groups are when the teacher simply organises groups by number of participants. Other types result from purposeful decisions made by the teacher. Each of these different types of grouping carries with it advantages and disadvantages which need to be considered when you decide on which sort of grouping to employ. Table 3.4 lists some of these.

Table 3.4 Advantages and disadvantages of group types

Group type	Advantages	Disadvantages
Friendship groups	• Established group dynamic • Pupils already know each other	• Reinforces existing social strata – leaders and followers • Possibility for off-task discussion Issue of those with limited social skills might not fit in

		• Can create outsiders if group numbers are limited
Ability groups	• Targeted support can be given • Possibility of high levels of achievement from some; can help gifted and talented (G&T) pupils not be distracted	• Ability is a problematic construct – is this just communication skills? • What are your criteria for choosing? • Social stigma and labelling e.g. 'the thick group' – might result
Structured mix	• Ensures no one is left out; reduces off-task chat • Allows for social engineering – weak with strong	• Time can be wasted establishing a social dynamic • Tends to establish leaders in that position • Quiet pupils can get 'swamped'
Random mix	• Allows pupils to establish new contacts • Has face validity (seems 'fair')	• As structured mix • Plus existing enmities can hinder progress
Single sex	• Can allow power to be equalised (i.e. boys don't get all the computers) • Can be within some pupils' comfort zones • Some minority ethnic cultures prefer it	• Can increase gender issues • Can result in needless inter-gender rivalries

There are obviously a number of issues in Table 3.4 where you need to have some knowledge of the class, especially of social dynamics and friendship matters, before you will be able to effectively organise meaningful groupings which will be able to function well. There is no straightforward answer as to which grouping is likely to produce the most effective results, as you can see from the *disadvantages* column. Friendship groups are used by many teachers as a way of allowing pupils to work within an established social dynamic.

RESEARCH SUMMARY RESEARCH SUMMARY **RESEARCH SUMMARY** RESEARCH SUMMARY

Kutnick et al. (2005) found that 81.6 per cent of friendship groups were of more or less the same ability. They also found that overtly grouping pupils by ability (other than by the effects of friendship groupings) could have an adverse effect on achievement:

Same ability grouping may also inhibit classroom learning, particularly when classroom tasks involve some form of cognitive discussion. Same ability groupings have been found to disadvantage certain pupils ... low ability groupings rarely have the range of cognitive perspectives that will allow discussions to develop and that high ability groupings rarely share information. (Kutnick et al., 2005)

An implication of this finding is that you need to think carefully before employing some form of ability-based grouping as to what possible and unintended effects might result.

There are also issues with employing purposive mixed-gender groups:

... studies have demonstrated that whilst boys and girls can work in groups, whether in separate or mixed groups, girls' style of interacting is different and tends to be more conflict-free, which is not necessarily positive from an educational point of view, particularly if it involves a disinclination to risk disrupting a group by exchanging contrasting views ... (Quicke and Winter, 1995)

Again, constituting a group of mixed boys and girls can cause issues which you need to be aware of beforehand.

However, the issues discussed in this section should not mean that organising groups is so fraught with dangers that you should not try. Simply ensure that you think through your organisational strategies before you begin. Discussing in advance how you will populate a group with your subject mentor, with LSAs or with other teachers will give you a lot of information as to which is the best way to proceed.

Metaphors for learning

Having begun with a consideration of theoretical issues and then discussed practical matters of classroom implementation, it is now time to join the two together.

Instead of theories of learning or knowledge, Sfard (1998) proposes two metaphors, the *acquisition* metaphor and the *participation* metaphor. In the acquisition metaphor knowledge and learning are treated in the manner of possessions, this *... brings to mind the activity of accumulating material goods* (Sfard, 1998, p5). In this way of looking at learning it is as if the learner has become the *owner* of these materials in that they have been *acquired* – hence *acquisition*.

In the participation metaphor what happens is that the learner is viewed as a person involved in *participation in certain kinds of activities rather than in accumulating private possessions* (Sfard, 1998, p6). This metaphor involves the learner being involved and actively participating.

Sfard goes on to say that the metaphors are not designed to be exclusive, and that a logical stance for the classroom practitioner is to employ a mixture of the two:

> An adequate combination of the acquisition and participation metaphors would bring to the fore the advantages of each, while keeping their respective drawbacks at bay.

> (Sfard, 1998, p11)

For you, these metaphors provide a useful way of thinking about, and describing in your planning and reflection materials, what is taking place in your classroom.

> **REFLECTIVE TASK**
>
> Think about a learning activity that you taught or observed recently. How much of it can be described by the *participation* metaphor and how much by the *acquisition*?

Using the metaphors in teaching for creativity

In deciding what you and your pupils will be doing when you undertake creative teaching and learning activities in your classroom, the *acquisition* and *participation* metaphors will help with categorising learning and doing. It is likely that in any lesson or unit of work you will have aspects of learning which you wish the pupils to possess – to acquire – and there will be moments when you wish the pupils to participate.

Teaching example – Key Stage 3 Science

As an example let us take a very straightforward science lesson experiment where pupils are required to boil a liquid in a test tube over a Bunsen burner, take a temperature measurement, pour the liquid into a container, allow it to cool for two minutes and finally measure the temperature again. Some of the knowledge for this task needs to be *possessed* by the pupils, health and safety issues being a prime example, but also how to know when the liquid is boiling, what the concept of temperature entails, how to record a reading of it, and the like. All of this knowledge is accounted for by the acquisition metaphor. The participation metaphor accounts for the way the activity is done, as a corporate endeavour with two or more pupils working cooperatively and *doing* practical work together, including knowledge of how to connect and assemble the apparatus, how to measure the temperature using a thermometer, how to say the reading so that another pupil can record it, how to pour the liquid from one container to another, and so on.

PRACTICAL TASK PRACTICAL TASK **PRACTICAL TASK** PRACTICAL TASK **PRACTICAL TASK**

Plan an activity for a lesson you will be teaching soon, and account for aspects of the learning that will take place using the two metaphors in a similar fashion to the science experiment described above.

Conclusion

In this chapter we have considered theoretical and practical approaches to teaching for creativity. Working through the material in this section will help you consider how to plan for your own pedagogy to develop with regard to teaching for creativity. Although we have provided you with step-by-step assistance what we cannot do is provide a 'one size fits all' template for you to use. This is because:

> You cannot follow a recipe for developing creativity – first because there is none; second because such a recipe would provide uncreative *role modelling*.

(Sternberg and Williams, 1996, p8)

All contexts and situations are different and so we have emphasised *planning* for teaching for creativity, as you will be able to fill in the gaps with your knowledge of the context, the school, pupils, classrooms, resources, timings, prior knowledge and so on, and be able to act as a *creative* role model for your classes.

A SUMMARY OF **KEY POINTS**

> **Planning for creativity** – devising lesson plans for lessons which plan in creative activities.

> **Types of knowledge** – how different type of knowledge impact on the creative process.

> **Learning and task outcomes** – what these are, and why learning is important.

> **Writing learning outcomes** – not easy to do, but need to be considered separately from task outcomes.

> Questioning – how to use questioning to take pupil knowledge forward.

> Bloom's taxonomy – categorising questions based on cognitive activity.

> Revision adding *creativity* to higher level thinking in Bloom's taxonomy.

> Question stems – how to use these to write questions which take pupil learning forward.

> Possibility thinking (Craft) – thinking tangentially.

> Metacognition – thinking about thinking, and how to develop it using ...

> Questioning for metacognition – the importance of modelling good questioning.

> Wait time – give the pupils time to think.

> Group learning – different ways of organising pupils into groups.

> The zone of proximal development – achievement increased by working socially.

> Multiple intelligences – not just a single IQ figure.

> Activity theory – looking at the way in which people cooperate, and the effect of mediating artefacts.

> Acquisition and participation metaphors – not theories of learning but ways individuals own or participate in knowledge and creative processes.

> You as role model for creativity – what you say, and what questions you ask.

REFERENCES REFERENCES **REFERENCES** REFERENCES **REFERENCES** REFERENCES

Anderson, L.W. and Krathwohl, D.R. (2001) *A taxonomy for learning, teaching, and assessing: a revision of Bloom's taxonomy of educational objectives*. New York and London: Longman.

Black, P., Harrison, C. Lee, C., Marshall, B. and Wiliam, D. (2004) Working inside the black box. *Phi Delta Kappan*, 86, 8–21.

Bloom, B.S. (1956) *Taxonomy of educational objectives. Handbook I: the cognitive domain*. New York: David McKay.

Cole, M. and Engestrom, Y. (1993) A cultural-historical approach to distributed cognition. In Salomon, G. (ed), *Distributed cognitions*. Cambridge: Cambridge University Press.

Craft, A. (2000) *Creativity across the primary curriculum: framing and developing practice*. London: Routledge.

Craft, A. (2001) Little c creativity. In Craft, A., Jeffrey, B. and Leibling, M. (eds), *Creativity in education*. London: Continuum.

Craft, A. (2005) *Creativity in schools – tensions and dilemmas*. Abingdon: Routledge.

Crozier, J. (2004) Positive approaches to supporting pupil behaviour. In Brooks, V., Abbott, I. and Bills, L. (eds), *Preparing to teach in secondary schools*. Maidenhead: Open University Press.

Daniels, H. (2001) *Vygotsky and pedagogy*. London: RoutledgeFalmer.

DfES (2001) *Literacy across the curriculum: Key Stage 3 strategy*. London: DfES.

DfES (2002) *Training materials for the foundation subjects*. London: DfES.

DfES (2003) *Key messages – pedagogy and practice*. Online at: **www.standards.dfes.gov.uk/ keystage3/downloads/ks3_km2003.pdf**

Gardner, H. (1983) *Frames of mind*. London: Heinemann.

Gardner, H. (1999) Assessment in context. In Murphy, P. (ed), *Learners, learning and assessment*. London: Paul Chapman in association with Open University.

John, P. (2006) Lesson planning and the student teacher: re-thinking the dominant model. *Journal of Curriculum Studies,* 38 (4), 483–98.

Koestler, A. (1964) *The act of creation*. London: Macmillan.

Kutnick, P., Blatchford, P. and Baines, E. (2005) Grouping of pupils in secondary school classrooms: possible links between pedagogy and learning. *Social Psychology of Education*, 8 (4), 349–74.

Lave, J. and Wenger, E. (1991) *Situated learning: legitimate peripheral participation*. Cambridge: Cambridge University Press.

OFSTED (2003) *Expecting the unexpected: developing creativity in primary and secondary schools*. Online at: **www.ofsted.gov.uk**

Palincsar, A.M., Brown, A.L. and Campione, J.C. (1993) First-grade dialogues for knowledge acquisition and use. In Forman, E.A., Minick, N. and Stone, C.A. (eds), *Contexts for learning: sociocultural dynamics in children's development*. New York: Oxford University Press, pp43–57.

Polanyi, M. (1967) *The tacit dimension*. London: Routledge & Kegan Paul.

Quicke, J. and Winter, C. (1995) 'Best friends': a case-study of girls' reactions to an intervention designed to foster collaborative group work. *Gender and Education,* 7 (3), 259–82.

Robinson, K. (2001) *Out of our minds: learning to be creative*. Oxford: Capstone.

Roth, W.-M. (1999) Authentic school science. In McCormick, R. and Paechter, C. (eds), *Learning and knowledge*. London: Paul Chapman.

Rowe, M.B. (1974) Wait-time and rewards as instructional variables. *Journal of Research in Science Teaching*, 11, 81–94.

Runco, M. (2003) Education for creative potential. *Scandinavian Journal of Educational Research*, 47, 317–24.

Ryle, G. (1949) *The concept of mind*. Harmondsworth: Penguin Books.

Salomon, G. (1993) No distribution without individuals' cognition: a dynamic interactional view. In Salomon, G. (ed), *Distributed cognitions*. Cambridge: Cambridge University Press.

Sawyer, R.K. (2003) *Group creativity: music, theater, collaboration*. Mahwah, NJ: Lawrence Erlbaum.

Sfard, A. (1998) On two metaphors for learning and the dangers of choosing just one. *Educational Researcher*, 27 (2), 4–13.

Sternberg, R. and Williams, W.M. (1996) *How to develop student creativity*. Alexandria, VA: ASCD.

Vygotsky, L. (1978) *Mind in society*. Cambridge, MA: Harvard University Press.

4
Creative learning – learning to think in new ways

By the end of this chapter you should:

- **have thought about what learning is and what it entails;**
- **have considered what is going when learning takes place;**
- **have reflected on what the contribution of creativity is to learning;**
- **have thought about what makes creative learning different from other types of learning.**

This chapter will help you to meet the following Professional Standards for QTS:
Q1, Q7, Q8, Q10, Q15, Q22, Q25, Q29, Q30, Q31

Introduction

This chapter investigates the main issues from the overall diagram, as shown in Figure 4.1.

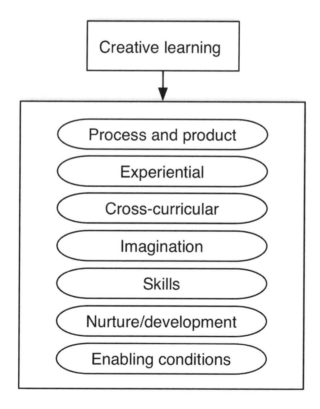

Fig. 4.1. Chapter 4: overview

Views of learning

In Chapter 1 we considered the nature of learning under three headings – behaviourist, cognitive and situated. Even within the broad family of cognitive views there are considerable differences. At one end of the spectrum stands the rationalist view. This states that learning is about mapping reality onto the mind of the learner. This gives rise to a view that:

> ... knowledge representing how the world really is must be transmitted to the students. It is then presumed that when they have the same statements in their heads as the teacher has or as appear in the book they know something.
> (Bredo, 1999, p28)

It is this view which is often characterised as being the 'chalk and talk' view of education. It also gives rise to the staffroom saying 'they must know it by now, I've taught it to them hundreds of times'.

Contrasting with the rationalist view of learning is the constructivist view, which we introduced in Chapter 1. In this view learners make meanings for themselves – they are not simply trying to get a version of reality inside their heads.

> Within education, constructivist ideas are translated as meaning that all learners actually construct knowledge for themselves, rather than knowledge coming from the teacher and being 'absorbed' by the pupil. This means that every pupil will learn something slightly different from a given lesson, and that as a teacher we can never be certain what our pupils will learn. (Muijs and Reynolds, 2005, p62)

Learning, viewed in this way, is about the individual *creating* meanings for themselves. Within the cognitive family, creative learning is more likely to figure towards the constructivist end of the spectrum, where pupils *make* meanings for themselves. Muijs and Reynolds make another useful point in this extract, that of the teacher not knowing what the pupils will learn. You will have learning outcomes for your lessons, but even so it is highly likely that your pupils will learn things for which you have not legislated!

Process and product

In creative learning we expect the pupils to be actively involved in the *process* of learning. In the 'chalk and talk' view of learning it is the end *product* of learning which is deemed to be important, or, as Bredo (1999) put it, the pupil *having the same statements in their heads as the teacher*. In this view, valuing the product is often achieved by devaluing the process; it is the resultant knowledge in the heads of the pupils which is the focus of attention, and either it is there or it isn't. In creative learning we are often as concerned with process as with product; in other words it is the *journey* which matters as much as the *destination*. However, this is not to say that creativity and learning are the same thing, nor that there is no place for the rationalist position. There are occasions when we want pupils to know established facts and have them ready to recall – we do not want children having to discover for themselves what the two times table is each time they need it; neither, on a more adult level, do we want learner drivers experimenting with passing a red traffic light to see what happens. Having a focus on process is something that creative learning entails and which is undertaken *purposefully*.

This focus of attention on process is one which has come to the fore in recent years:

> *A shift to process has been characteristic of recent work on both creativity and development.* (Sawyer, 2003, p36)

Creative learning is not a gimmick to amuse pupils: its purpose is to connect *learning* with *knowing*. It is also worth emphasising that creative learning is about *learning*. A casual observer looking in on a creative learning project in action might assume it is about *doing*. Activity is involved, but *doing* is the servant of *learning*, not its master.

Four key elements of creative learning

But what does this mean for you in the classroom? How can you consider learning and then decide what sort of activities you should establish to aim for in creative learning?

There are four key elements to this:

- **Divergent thinking – developing imagination.**
- **Experiential learning – developing and accumulating experiences.**
- **Motivation – fostering an on-task mentality in the pupils, springing from ...**
- **Enjoyment – undertaking creative learning should be fun!**

Starting at the bottom of this list, creative learning can motivate pupils as it will be seen as a change from the routine activities of learning. A lesson which the pupils see as fun cannot be a bad thing:

> *... in a school system where we are often plagued by our children's disaffection and a lack of engagement, surely letting them have a bit of fun is a really, really good idea.* (Cowley, 2005, p7)

Where motivation can be increased, then all sorts of potentially beneficial spin-offs follow.

Moving to the first item now, fostering divergent thinking (see Chapter 1) is a good way to begin to address creative learning.

PRACTICAL TASK PRACTICAL TASK **PRACTICAL TASK** PRACTICAL TASK **PRACTICAL TASK**

Starter activities

In all subjects areas, a good way to gently introduce creative learning is as a starter activity. Find a picture (look in Sunday supplements/magazines/the internet) which is tangential to your subject area and ask the pupils what the picture is about. Emphasise that there might not be any right or wrong answers! Thus in history a picture of an eye could herald a lesson in a sequence on the Norman Conquest, representing how Harold was killed. In Citizenship a picture of an empty car boot could introduce a discussion about people smuggling across borders. In English an image featured as a metaphor in a poem studied could be used.

All of the starter activities listed above are developing the imagination and that is a key component of creative learning.

Experiential learning

Experiential learning is another area where creativity can be promoted. We know that pupils learn from doing, and situated learning theorists such as Lave and Wenger (1991) tell us that there is learning which arises from social participation in group activities. We would not want to teach team sports by only working with individuals and the same can be true in other subject areas too. Experiencing things in a new way can result in deeper learning.

Teaching examples – some established ideas

Role plays: these have been used in many contexts for a long time. Have you tried them? Why not get a group of pupils to role play something in your subject. Drama, English and MFL teachers have been doing this, and will have expertise you can draw on if you are just starting out.

Dummy microphone: have an unplugged microphone, only the person with the microphone can speak; the others have to wait for their turn.

Hotseating: pupils take it in turns to be in the hotseat to be asked questions on a topic being studied by the class. For variety try this with the hotseat only able to answer 'yes' or 'no'.

Some of these ideas may seem a little bizarre compared with strait-laced lessons you have observed. Creativity can be associated with wackiness and sometimes an 'off the wall' idea can be used for a lesson or a series of lessons.

PRACTICAL TASK PRACTICAL TASK PRACTICAL TASK PRACTICAL TASK PRACTICAL TASK

Try some wacky ideas

What could the pupils do with some balloons?

What would a collage of newspaper headlines look like?

What could the pupils do with some pieces of string and bits of wood?

Could the pupils tell a story in song lyrics?

Experience is cumulative. We want our pupils to build on what they have done before, and so we will want to sequence activities so that we are not just providing a series of 'one-offs'. This too is a part of creative learning. Teachers often have a list of skills and concepts that they would like their pupils to have learned or be able to do by the end of a unit of work. The convergent thinking approach to teaching skills and concepts would be to work through them in a sequential fashion, teaching a specific skill and then applying it later. As a creative learning alternative, some teachers have tried setting up tasks in which the pupils then need to learn or develop the necessary skills to be able to achieve. Green (2002) has written of the skills developed informally in order to play pop and rock music. In this case the task often precedes skill acquisition.

REFLECTIVE TASK
REFLECTIVE TASK

Think of a series of skills or concepts in your subject area. What ways are there you can establish a task that requires the learning of these 'on the job'?

This method of working is a more authentic way of teaching and learning in that a real-world situation forms the basis for what is going on. Authentic tasks form a way for pupils to become engaged with learning because there is a real purpose to what they are doing.

Teaching example – Practising skills

In one secondary school, instead of hypothetically writing articles for a newspaper, the pupils were engaged with all aspects of production, from writing via desktop publishing to printing and distributing the finished product. This gave them ownership of all stages in the work they were doing and required them to learn and practise skills which would otherwise have been taught in isolation.

Cross-curricular links

This takes us to another aspect of creative learning, the possibility of forming links between curriculum subject areas. Some projects which lend themselves to creative learning techniques are genuinely cross-curricular and utilise skills, techniques and knowledge from different disciplines. Many schools have used time 'off timetable' for projects such as this.

Teaching example – Citizenship

In another secondary school Citizenship projects were conceived of in an off-timetable manner. One project was to plan for the construction of a new play area for an infant school in the area. This involved researching what the younger children wanted in their play area, then finding out about health and safety issues, planning permission, equipment availability and so on. This was an authentic task with tangible results.

These two vignettes demonstrate key elements of creative learning. According to Hobbs, the two key elements required in a creative learning project are *imagination* and *experience*:

> *Creative Learning is a process which focuses on students' ideas. Two things are key within this process: imagination and experience ... In the classroom, students take their own imagination as their starting point. They continually use and re-use their imagination, producing unique ideas for the completion of a classroom task. Students then act on those ideas singly and often in groups, learning how to bring them into manifestation via the acquisition of further relevant knowledge and skills. Lastly students also refine those ideas according to their practical experience with them in the classroom. Alongside they will have developed the knowledge they had already and taken on new skills.* (Hobbs, 2005)

New ways of working

In this way of working in creative learning, skills are acquired *in situ* as they are needed and used purposefully. This can involve a major change in pedagogy for some teachers. Returning to our discussion of skills and concepts, we know that teaching these forms an integral part of, and figure prominently in, many units of work. We have already discussed how established teachers have often portrayed a straightforward linear progression of skill acquisition for their classes and can be reluctant to deviate from these pre-existing structures they have created. Reasons for this might include:

- unwillingness to change tried and tested ways of working;
- fear of change;
- concerns over assessment;
- apprehension of reactions of colleagues;
- concern over impressions on headteacher and leadership team;
- fear of OFSTED responses;
- concerns about behaviour management.

However, every journey begins with a single step, and teachers who have changed their approach and adopted creative learning techniques have often found it liberating. For example, a science teacher who had been using a creative learning project with her pupils said:

> ... personally it's given me inspiration, its motivated me, it's made my job easier because the amount of behavioural issues I've experienced has gone down; it's also making the subject really positive to the students, I am also hoping in retrospect it might help raise attainment.

It is often a 'fear of letting go' that provides a real disincentive for teachers to try creative learning strategies, as

> ... teachers are extremely pragmatic ... and reluctant to abandon a teaching approach that has worked satisfactorily for them in the past ... Some teachers are wary of being too bold and imaginative because of the practical implications in respect of pupil behaviour, the time available for sessions, parental expectations, examination results and the like. They would like to be more creative 'in an ideal world' but will need to be convinced that there is sufficient evidence of the benefits that accrue. (Hayes, 2004)

However, as a new teacher you do not have the same 'baggage' as an established teacher, and it is worth being inventive at this stage in your practice. Indeed, many in-school mentors feel this is an important aspect of your role as trainee teacher or NQT. One well-established general mentor in a secondary school said:

> I like having trainee teachers, they have fresh ideas, and the enthusiasm to try them out. I want them to try new things, and if their ideas are a bit off-the-wall, that's fine by me; I'll support them all I can. They have a spin-off effect on the old hands [established teachers], and I often see little nuggets they've [the established teachers] picked up being used.

New teachers – new ideas!

Sometimes a trainee teacher or an NQT can be the spur into action an established teacher has been looking for in order to effect change. One subject mentor commented:

> I've had these units of work for about five years now, and I was getting fed up with teaching them, so having a trainee teacher made me say to her, 'right – you design your own stuff, and I'm happy to tidy it up' and this is what we did, and I'm really pleased with the results.

Letting go of the linear acquisition of skills can be harder though. There are close links with assessment here. However, as we shall discuss in Chapter 5, assessment of skills is relatively straightforward, and allows for evidencing progression in a tangible way. However, you need to remember that disentangling skill progression in units of work in the way we have been describing can, as the science teacher above noted, have a liberating effect on both teacher and pupils.

The place of skills in a unit of work

Music is often considered as a creative discipline per se, but even here there can be an insistence on a predetermined sequence of skill acquisition. To counter this, one music teacher taking part in an LEA project in an inner-city school spoke of how moving to a position where she was not teaching skills in advance but allowing pupils to compose their own music had changed her mind:

> *I was very wary at first, I thought they wouldn't cope, and it'd be chaos. I'd warned the SMT* [senior management team – the head and deputies] *that I was doing this, just in case. There was a bit of chaos at first, but then they* [the pupils] *settled down and got on with it ... I like the freedom of creativity they got. Before I would have structured it, but they all came up with something completely different. They wouldn't have come up with ideas like this from the previous way of working.*

Support of the SMT

Apprehension over colleagues' approval and responses from the SMT have made some teachers wary – the music teacher above felt it necessary to 'warn' colleagues that differences would be noted. Often teachers are surprised at the positive responses they get. They need not be so, as in many cases, heads and SMTs often welcome change, knowing that it can refresh staff and pupil enthusiasm for subjects. As the science teacher quoted above went on to say:

> *My headteacher has been really enthusiastic about it, he sees the difference it's making to the student. Generally they've* [the SMT] *been really supportive. At the end of the project I am doing a presentation to the SMT and the governors, we're trying to make changes to the curriculum in terms of teaching and learning styles across the board ...*

External inhibiting factors

Concerns about inspection and accountability can also negatively impact upon teachers:

> *... teachers' work is seen as increasingly dependent upon an externally imposed apparatus of behavioural objectives, assessment and accountability, leading to a proliferation of paperwork and administrative tasks, chronic work overload and the loss of opportunities for more creative work ...* (McNess et al., 2003)

This external pressure is often personified in the form of OFSTED inspections. We know that:

> *Some teachers perceive that Ofsted inspections create a climate of fear. They feel that they are expected to be doing something to satisfy Ofsted.* (Neesom, 2000)

This is a perception which OFSTED itself has worked at changing, and recognising the importance of creative learning experiences for pupils:

> ... *their* [the pupils] *perception of the learning environment ... was seen as more creative, allowing them to work through their thoughts, ideas and feelings. Little was perceived as 'wrong' and criticisms were seen as positively taking the work forward, developing 'mistakes' to creative advantage. The pupils felt that they received good feedback on their efforts and that this developed their sense of success and the possibility of further improvement. 'We have got teachers who say you can do it, not you can't. They boost our confidence and get us to aim higher'...* (OFSTED, 2003)

It is also to be hoped that with changing nature of school inspections, teachers will feel that there will be less of an emphasis on close scrutiny of individuals and that there will be greater latitude to initiate divergent thinking activities.

Imagination

In the extract cited above Hobbs (2005) pointed out the importance of *imagination*. For creative learning experiences, exercising the imagination is an important component, and it is *exercise* which is an important term. Developing the imagination of young people is not simply a piece of window-dressing as a side-effect to the main business of learning, it is an important skill in its own right. Transferable skills which result are those which are valued in situations beyond the immediate:

> *These transferable skills would include the ability to work flexibly, and respond and adapt to change; the ability to work both independently and within groups or teams; and the ability to build on and develop existing sets of professional skills and forms of knowledge.* (Hobbs, 2005)

To foster these skills among the young people in your classes, direct action is needed, they need to be nurtured and developed in a positive and deliberate fashion.

Nurturing and developing creative learning

Teaching example – capturing the imagination

We suggested some wacky ideas above – sometimes something that seems a little odd can grip the imagination of the young people in your classes. The first suggestion – balloons – was used by a French teacher in a school near the south coast. She asked her pupils to write down a question in French and attach it to a balloon which the pupils then released when the wind was in the right direction. Even if they didn't get any replies, the process of the activity made it far more memorable than if they had simply worked at the correct grammar for questions in the classroom.

PRACTICAL TASK PRACTICAL TASK **PRACTICAL TASK** PRACTICAL TASK **PRACTICAL TASK**

Extending thinking skills

As a starter activity, or an initial lesson in a creative learning unit of work, try asking the class to think in different ways.

- Can they make notes on a topic using only a picture?
- Can they make notes on a topic using only a series of symbols?
- Make notes on a topic using different 'traffic light' colours – red for important, amber for medium importance, green for not important, but interesting.
- Do they know what a mind map is? Can they use one?
- Read aloud a paragraph and ask the class to note only one word which sums it up for them.

PRACTICAL TASK PRACTICAL TASK PRACTICAL TASK PRACTICAL TASK PRACTICAL TASK

'What if'

Encourage divergent thinking by asking 'what if' questions.

- What if the Beatles hadn't met?
- What if television hadn't been invented?
- What if your eyes were in your stomach?
- What if we could see smells?
- What if we had four arms?
- What is gravity like on the Moon?

Some of these questions can be used purposefully to extend thinking, and can be used in all subjects to both extend thinking, and to challenge preconceptions.

Group work

We have discussed group work in earlier chapters, but it is equally important in creative learning, and tasks can be devised and set which are appropriate to be undertaken by groups of pupils. The skill of cooperation is not the only thing that will be fostered here, Vygotsky's notion of the *zone of proximal development* means that pupils working in groups will have the potential for achieving at a higher level than they would individually. In group creative learning projects the possibility also exists that 'many hands make light work', so working together on a common project means that the whole group will achieve at a higher level than that which its individual members might. In cognitive terms what is happening is that the creative process is being *distributed* between a number of individuals simultaneously:

> ... *resources that shape and enable activity are distributed in configuration across people, environments, and situations. In other words, intelligence is accomplished rather than possessed.* (Pea, 1993, p50)

In theoretical terms this is taking us towards *activity theory*, which investigates how people work cooperatively in groups. It takes a view of learning which is a long way from the rationalist stance which we looked at earlier:

> *[Activity theory] understands learning not as the internalisation of discrete information or skills by individuals, but rather as expanding involvement over time – social as well as intellectual – with other people and the tools available in their culture.* (Russell, 2004, p310)

From this theoretical position the important facet for you to take as a classroom teacher is the prominence it gives to group work. Creative learning projects which take place in groups are not done as a substitute for learning, they *are* the learning!

Organising creative learning in groups in the classroom

Many of the tasks we have discussed so far are group *activities*. There are times when you will want to set up a group creative learning task from the outset. Let us think through what goes on in a creative learning group activity, and work through some of the decisions you as teacher need to make.

Figure 4.2 is a graphical representation of the main elements of a creative learning project. It is important to keep in mind that prior learning and experiences are an important part of what is going on – creative learning does not arise out of nothing but should be seen as part of a *planned* sequence of events. It is worthwhile to note too that the creative learning project being planned will form part of the pupils' future prior learning too!

Fig. 4.2. Simple representation of the creative process

One of the early decisions you will need to make is whether the creative learning project you will be undertaking is to focus on *process* or *product*. There are then a whole series of decisions you need to work through in order to undertake your planning for a creative learning project, such as those included in Table 4.1.

Table 4.1 Criteria for creative learning group work projects

Decisions to be taken	Issues, comments and further questions
Learning outcomes	What are the intended learning outcomes for this project? Note these should be *learning* outcomes, not *task* outcomes.
Place in unit of work	Is this the right place for this creative learning activity? What have the pupils been doing before this, and what will they be doing next?
Influence of prior learning	Do they know what they need to know to start the creative learning activity?
Place of skills	Do they have the skills they need to start the creative learning activity? Do you expect them to need to learn more skills as they work through it? If so, what are they?
Nature of outcome, which will lead to ...	What is the end point of the activity?
Focus = process or product	Is there a clear choice? Is it the outcome that matters, or is it the process of getting there? Does the outcome matter at all, or are you solely interested in the process?

If product:

What will it be?	Is it a tangible artefact?
What will be done with it? Will it be assessed – if so, how?	Give some thought to this – how can it be shared with others? If it is to be assessed, what criteria will you be using? Will you establish these in advance? Will you share them with the pupils?
Will it be celebrated?	Is it expected to be something impressive? Will you want other pupils/teachers/the head/parents/governors/the community/the media to see it? Is it a performance event?
How important is the process? (see next ...)	Are you solely interested in the product? Does the process they go through matter, or do you want them to get rapidly to a point where they can have a tangible product?

If process:

What are the success criteria?	Will you establish these in advance?
Is group work itself a successful outcome?	If your objective is, say, social skills, then are these your success criteria? How will you deal with pupils who have difficulty working in groups, or where social issues arise?
How much teacher/adult intervention is appropriate?	How much help do you want to give to the creative process? How will you deal with off-task behaviour? How much steering towards solutions will you give? What sort of formative assessments and feedback are appropriate?
What will the endpoint be?	How will you know, if the focus is on process, what will the outcome be? And ...
How will you know when it has been reached?	... how will you arrive at a decision about at what point they will have finished, and you wish to move on?
If there is a product, what will happen to it? (see *product* questions above)	If the process is the important thing but still results in a product, what will happen to that product?
Will the process be assessed – if so, how?	What will the success criteria be? Co-operation? Teamwork? Ideas? On-task-ness?
Type of activity that will be undertaken	What will the pupils actually be doing?
Duration of task	For how long do you anticipate the task running?
Provision for overrunning?	What will you do if the pupils take longer than you anticipate for the task? What are the knock-on effects for the next unit of work or, if you are on a school placement, will you have to leave before it is finished?
Contingency plans for underrunning?	What are your plans if it does not take as long as you have planned?
What will you do if some finish earlier than others?	Will you have a strategy in place to deal with this, or will you get them to make further refinements or undertake some form of evaluation?
Nature and constitution of groups that will be employed	See section on *group work*. How will you decide on the constitution of the groups you establish? Will friendship groups work, or others?
If more than one group, how will the teacher/other adults divide their time?	How will you monitor, give feedback, assist and be of use to the groups? Are there other adults in the classroom – e.g. LSAs, learning mentors, subject mentors – how will you deploy these to good effect?
How will roles within the groups be allocated?	Will you tell them what roles should be filled? Let them find out? Let them choose?

Materials required?	What do you and the pupils need? Have you got it? Is there a budget? Is it realistic? Will anyone sponsor it?
Timetabling issues?	Will the project need more time than timetabled lessons? If so, how will it be organised?
Importance of continuity – what will happen to pupils if key members are absent?	Will the other members of the group be unable to work? What plans can you make to deal with this?

Working through these questions, and thinking carefully about the issues, should give you a good starting point from which to begin planning a creative learning project with a class. As a planning pro forma, using the questions in the left-hand column and then writing your own planning responses in the right-hand column will give you a template to include in your planning file.

Within-lesson creative learning

However, not all creative learning projects need to happen over time, and it is equally possible to undertake creative learning episodes within a lesson which do not involve the same level of planning as that shown in Table 4.1. For these within-lesson creative learning episodes many of the same types of decision need to be made, but made within the context of a single lesson or as episodes within a series of lessons. The planning schedule for this is shown as a decision-making flowchart in Figure 4.3. In this flowchart abbreviated headings from the questions in Table 4.1 have been used. Working through this flowchart should help you to begin planning episodic creative learning activities.

Success criteria

It is clear from both Table 4.1 and Figure 4.3 that success criteria need to be decided for some of the stages in the work the pupils do. This is useful for you to establish in your mind, and will help you prevent your pupils from getting stuck. It may be helpful if these success criteria are drafted out in advance, then you can make a decision on whether you can share them with the pupils. Here are some possible examples of success criteria that are meant to be shared:

- **The planning should include a list of who is doing what job.**
- **Once you have painted the background, let me know.**
- **The initial drawings need to be checked by Miss Smith**
- **The knots in the rope have to be tight enough to hold a 2 kg weight – test them and show me.**
- **The list of songs needs to last eleven minutes – enter the timings into Excel and show Danny.**
- **The sponsors have said you can have £35 worth of materials from their catalogue. Add up the figures and show me.**
- **Does it float?**
- **Question 20 people in the shopping centre. When you have analysed the results, show me.**

These success criteria often relate to task completion and it may well be that your creative learning requires sequencing in some way like this. For example, if they are designing a raft to float across the swimming pool and it sinks on being put into water then there is no point continuing – redesign is needed!

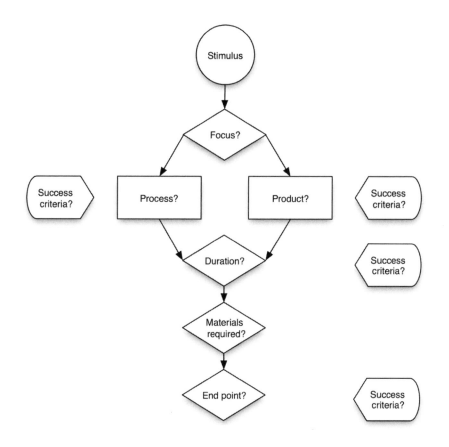

Fig. 4.3. Decision-making process for smaller projects

Whatever your creative learning project is going to be, having worked through the questions for the two outlines above, it should now be clear that Figure 4.2 was a very simplistic representation and that the process involved in a group creative task is likely to be more complex. The central component of the creative process is normally iterative in nature and involves planning, trying things out (where appropriate) and rethinking. Figure 4.4 makes this iterative process clearer.

What this means is that the pupils will need to spend a considerable amount of time planning and having ideas, and doing this over and over again. The old adage that creativity is 1 per cent inspiration and 99 per cent perspiration holds true here! You will need to allow time for thinking to take place, and space for the pupils to develop their ideas. The central part of the process looks circular and that is how it is best perceived, with ideas, planning aspects and trial-and-error applications being attempted. This is a key part of the creative process and again needs space and nurturing for it to occur.

Enabling conditions for creative learning

This brings us to the final consideration that we need to make when planning for creative learning, that of ensuring that *enabling conditions* are in place in order for creativity to occur.

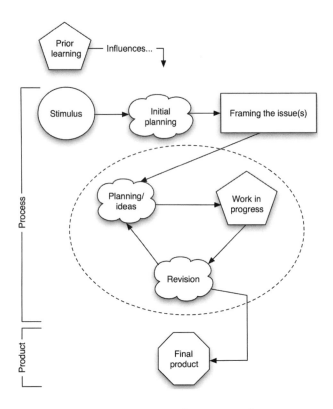

Fig. 4.4. Iterative nature of group creative process

Robinson (2001, pp128–9) outlines aspects of the creative process he describes as 'essential', one of these being: *the need for freedom to experiment and take risks.*

We need to ensure that pupils have the freedom – the 'space' as we said above – to try out their ideas and to undertake trial-and-error processes. Trial and error involves *error* – going wrong. Creative learning projects need to build in *the freedom to fail*. It is crucial that your creative learning projects include this. In the final analysis the pupils need space to experiment – and if they cannot keep all the metaphorical plates spinning, in the context of the classroom it does not matter! Risk taking needs to be a key part of creativity. As the old adage goes, you can't make an omelette without breaking a few eggs! To set up conditions for freedom may involve different classroom organisations, different ways of working and different teacher–pupil relationships. Hopefully the outlines of creative learning we have discussed so far will allow you to establish enabling conditions for your classes to be able to work at your projects with the freedom to succeed, but which also allow the possibility of not succeeding with good grace! Another old saying is 'expect success, plan for failure'.

In establishing creative learning projects you, as a teacher, are also being creative – and you too need space for this, including space to fail! Sometimes creative learning projects do not work. As a beginning teacher this can be a worrying prospect, but beware of being too staid, too 'safe' and not trying new things out! Headteachers and SMTs know this and will be aware that encouraging innovation involves risks too:

... for teachers the school climate must be one that welcomes innovation and accepts occasional reverses as an inevitable consequence of having an enterprising spirit ... Teachers must not be frozen in the headlights of performance targets or threats about the dire consequences of trying something new, but need opportunity to dream and imagine the potential advantages available to them. (Hayes, 2004)

In schools that encourage creative learning heads and SMTs will work hard to ensure that the 'school climate' nurtures this way of working. Your role is to facilitate learning, and creative learning enables the pupils to construct their own meanings from the work that they do. Creative learning is often deep learning.

Conclusion

Creative learning involves pupils in making new conditions, in active learning experiences and in having space and time to think, create and try out their ideas. This section has led you through the creative learning process, and discussed ways in which you can begin to plan for creative learning activities in your classroom.

A SUMMARY OF **KEY POINTS**

> **Views of learning** – we have considered how constructivist views can be allied closely with creative processes.

> **Process–product dichotomy** – we have considered whether creative learning will focus on process or product.

> **Divergent thinking** – fostering this has been seen as key to creativity.

> **Fun** – creative learning projects should be this!

> **Wacky** – sometimes 'off-the-wall' ideas can really grab the imagination of the pupils.

> **Freedom to try out new ideas** – there is no time like the present – why not give some these ideas a fair trial?

> **Approval of the SMT and OFSTED** – a common perception is that 'the powers that be' will not approve. We have seen that this is not the case.

> **Developing imagination** – this is what creative learning is all about.

> **Group work** – we have investigated in some detail how this is a key element of creative learning.

> **The need for prior learning to be taken into account.**

> **Success criteria** – it helps if you have some idea as to what these are before you begin a creative learning project.

> **Iterative nature of creative process** – much of the central part of the creative process is one which repeats itself. You need to allow space and time for this to happen.

> **Enabling conditions** – allow your pupils – and yourself – freedom to succeed, but space to fail.

REFERENCES REFERENCES **REFERENCES** REFERENCES **REFERENCES** REFERENCES

Bredo, E. (1999) Reconstructing educational psychology. In Murphy, P. (ed), *Learners, learning and assessment*. London: Paul Chapman.

Cowley, S. (2005) *Getting the buggers to be creative*. London: Continuum.

Green, L. (2002) *How popular musicians learn: a way ahead for music education*. London and New York: Ashgate.

Hayes, D. (2004) Understanding creativity and its implications for schools. *Improving Schools*, 7 (3), 279–86.

Hobbs, J. (2005) Why is creative learning so important? Available at: **http://www.schoolsnetwork.org.uk/uploads/documents/Why%20creative%20Learning%20is%20%important_119758.doc** (accessed 2 August 2006).

Lave, J. and Wenger, E. (1991) *Situated learning: legitimate peripheral participation*. Cambridge: Cambridge University Press.

McNess, E., Broadfoot, P. and Osborn, M. (2003) Is the effective compromising the affective? *British Educational Research Journal*, 29 (2), 243–57.

Muijs, D. and Reynolds, D. (2005) *Effective teaching: evidence and practice*. London: Sage.

Neesom, A. (2000) *Report on teachers' perceptions of formative assessment*. London: QCA.

OFSTED (2003) *Improving city schools: how the Arts can help*. London: OFSTED.

Pea, R. (1993) Practices of distributed intelligence and designs for education. In Salomon, G. (ed), *Distributed cognitions*. Cambridge: Cambridge University Press.

Robinson, K. (2001) *Out of our minds: learning to be creative*. Oxford: Capstone.

Russell, D.R. (2004) Looking beyond the interface: activity theory and distributed learning. In Daniels, H. and Edwards, A. (eds), *The RoutledgeFalmer reader in psychology of education*. London: RoutledgeFalmer.

Sawyer, R.K. (2003) *Creativity and development*. New York: Oxford University Press.

5
Assessment and creativity

By the end of this chapter you should:

- have thought about the nature and purpose of how you can use assessment with regard to creativity and creative acts;
- understand differences between formative and summative assessment;
- know how to use formative and summative assessment strategies to take the learning of your pupils forward;
- realise that your verbal comments made to pupils are important;
- have practised your skills in giving appropriate feedback to pupils engaged on creative tasks;
- have thought about the place of assessment in your consideration of creative processes and creative products.

This chapter will help you to meet the following Professional Standards for QTS:

Q1, Q6, Q7, Q10, Q11, Q12, Q18, Q19, Q22, Q25, Q26, Q27, Q28, Q29

Introduction

This chapter investigates the main issues from the overall diagram, as shown in Figure 5.1

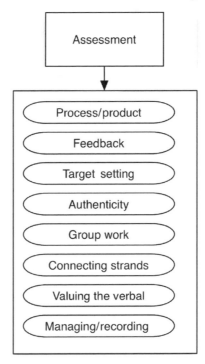

Fig. 5.1 Chapter 5: overview

This chapter considers what assessment is, what it has to offer teaching and learning with regard to creativity and how it can be undertaken on a day-to-day basis in your classroom.

Historically, particularly in the United States, it was not uncommon for creativity to be assessed as a single characteristic of an individual. Tests for creativity were devised which ranged from the scientific, based on psychometric principles (e.g. Torrance, 1966) to the wacky ('describe twenty uses for brick'). In the UK creativity tests were, and are, less common. Nowadays we are far more concerned with pupils working at tasks which have some degree of authenticity about them. Teachers have found that having a score of, say, 15/20 on a creativity test does not really tell them anything useful about the individual, whereas undertaking practical tasks in the classroom can be a far more meaningful activity.

To consider assessment in the context of creativity, we need to begin by thinking about a number of questions.

- **What is assessment?**
- **What is being assessed?**
- **Why is it being assessed?**
- **What will be done with the assessment information?**
- **What is the connection between assessment, learning and creativity?**

What is assessment?

It may seem that this first question is one which has an obvious response, along the lines of 'marking pupils' work', but it is not as straightforward as that, and developing an under-standing of assessment is key to thinking about the subsequent questions. What we can say is that assessment involves making judgements, evaluating pupil responses in some way and considering what can be done next for an individual or a group. Assessment should be at the centre of what takes place in schools:

> *Promoting children's learning is a principal aim of schools. Assessment lies at the heart of this process. It can provide a framework in which educational objectives may be set, and pupil's progress charted and expressed. It can yield a process for planning the next educational steps in response to children's needs. By facilitating dialogue between teachers, it can enhance professional skills and help the school as a whole to strengthen learning across the curriculum and throughout its age range. It should be an integral part of the educational process ... incorporated systematically into teaching strategies and practices at all levels.* (TGAT, 1988)

There are two main types of assessment which we talk about and use – these are *formative assessment* and *summative assessment*. The differences between the two are hinted at in their names. Summative assessment, to put it simply, *sums up* information about a pupil and presents it, often in the form of an examination grade. Thus A level grades are summative. Formative assessment *forms* an opinion as to what to do next to help the learner with their understanding or achievement. Formative assessment is also known as assessment *for* learning, or AfL, while summative assessment is also known as assessment *of* learning.

In your day-to-day work in the classroom you will make many decisions, and the quotation from the TGAT report above points towards one of the key areas, that of 'promoting chil-dren's learning'. As you teach a class, pupils will naturally make progress at different rates, are likely to achieve things at different speeds, and tend to work differently depending on whether they work alone or as part of a team. To promote the learning of your pupils, you need to have a view as to what they can do, both individually and collectively, and what it would be useful for them to do next. This takes us to the next of the key questions.

What is being assessed?

In Chapters 2, 3 and 4 we considered the different meanings and interpretations of the terms *teaching for creativity*, *teaching creatively* and *creative learning*, and we considered the tensions that exist between *creative processes* and *creative products*. As a teacher you will often be concerned with creative processes, and it is for these processes that formative assessment is going to be the most useful and appropriate tool. Indeed, many research findings support the notion that, properly used, formative assessment strategies can make a great deal of difference to results obtained in summatively assessed examinations later on (Black and Wiliam, 1998). In contexts of creative learning or teaching for creativity, it is often the case that pupils will be constructing new meanings for themselves. You will want to know whether these new meanings are being constructed effectively, and what and whether your pupils are learning from what they do. This will involve you making a judgement; this judgement will be a formative assessment. Formative assessment, then, is an area which can make a real difference to classroom learning, and what is likely to be assessed, in this instance, are creative processes.

It is important at this stage to consider the clear distinctions which exist between formative and summative assessment. Summative assessment ... *serves to inform an overall judgement on achievement* (Black, 1999, p118), while formative assessment ... *is concerned with the short term collection and use of evidence for the guidance of learning, mainly in day to day classroom practice* (ibid.). Summative assessment is concerned with certification and looking back over pupil achievement. It measures, it tests and it grades, and for these reasons summative assessment regimes are often called 'high-stakes' assessments, because examination grades matter and a lot can rest upon them. High-stakes assessments can also be used for purposes far wider than certification of pupil levels of achievement. For example, school league tables, openly available and published in newspapers, are constructed from data concerning pupil performance in tests at the end of key stages.

For our purposes in considering the role of assessment and creativity in the classroom, summative assessment will apply when products of creative processes are graded, for example at GCSE level, when many subjects require the submission of examples of pupil work as part of a portfolio of achievement. Often these products are graded solely on the evidence of the finished product, the artefact or performance itself. Creative processes tend to be underrepresented in grading systems in public examinations.

Figure 5.2 represents the different areas of attention for summative and formative assessment. The time-line along the bottom demonstrates progression from left to right, showing that summative assessment ignores future achievement by the pupil/s and concerns itself solely with documentation and certification of achievement. You can also see how summative assessment is separated from learning, and from achievement in the classroom. As Graue notes:

> ... *assessment and instruction are often conceived as curiously separate in both time and purpose.* (Graue, 1993, p291)

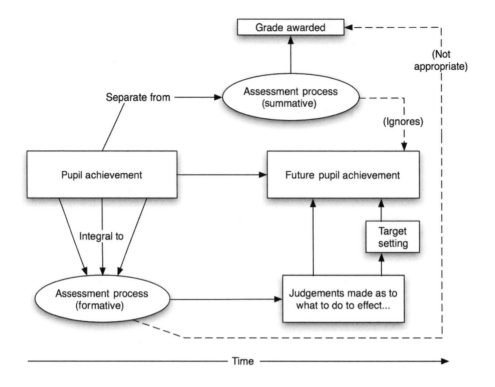

Fig. 5.2. Formative and summative assessment

In contrast to this, the lower portion of the diagram shows that formative assessment is occurring throughout the learning and doing stage of pupil achievement. It also shows that information gained during this stage is then used by the teacher, working in consultation with the pupils, to decide on the most efficacious course of action to take with regard to future learning and doing. Creative processes, whether classifiable as creative learning or teaching for creativity, will involve you and your pupils in formative assessment conversations regarding progress and future direction. These formative assessment conversations are, or should be, dialogues; it is important to emphasise that this is not the teacher holding a monologue! The reason that this notion of dialogue has been stressed is that it is during conversations that decisions which underpin actions that have been taken on the part of the pupils can emerge, and these are helpful in clarifying thought processes and thinking skills adopted and utilised by the pupil. Notice too that certification of achievement is not appropriate when using formative assessment.

Teaching example – Key Stage 3 Art

In an art class at Key Stage 3, the teacher was concerned about the drawing skills of some pupils. She got the class to draw one of their shoes, and went round the class talking to individual pupils as they did the task to find out what they were doing and why they were approaching the task in the way they were. This told her a lot. At the end of the task she then modelled the task herself, using phrases she heard the pupils themselves employ. She then used examples of pictures drawn by the pupils to engage them in reflection about what was a good outcome.

Feedback

Another aspect of formative assessment which it is important to consider from the perspective of creative work in the classroom is that of feedback. Feedback is a part of the dialogic process we have been discussing, in that it involves a conversation between pupil and teacher that is centred on helping the pupils understand what they are doing and, importantly, what they can do next. Used appropriately, feedback can make a great deal of difference to pupil achievement:

> *Feedback has been shown to improve learning where it gives each pupil specific guidance on strengths and weaknesses.* (Black and Wiliam, 1998)

Tunstall and Gipps investigated the feedback comments made by teachers and found they could be placed on a continuum, with descriptive comments at one end and evaluative comments at the other. What teachers said during these stages varied too:

> *At the evaluative end of the continuum, feedback is clearly either positive or negative. At the descriptive end, feedback can no longer be defined in these terms and is achievement or improvement focused.* (Tunstall and Gipps, 1996)

PRACTICAL TASK PRACTICAL TASK **PRACTICAL TASK** PRACTICAL TASK **PRACTICAL TASK**

Giving feedback is a skill which you are likely to have to practise, both as a trainee and as a newly qualified teacher, in order to become confident.

In lesson observations, look for instances where an experienced teacher is giving feedback to a group of pupils. What sorts of things do they say? Is it *evaluative*, *descriptive*, or somewhere between the two?

In your own teaching, next time you have a conversation where you give feedback to a group of pupils working on a topic in one of your classes, think about whether what you say is descriptive, evaluative or a mixture of both.

What do you find yourself saying?

Why are you saying it?

What do you hope will happen as a result of what you said?

Target setting

In Figure 5.2 the box in the lower right-hand corner of the diagram is labelled 'Judgements made as to what to do to effect ...' which is linked to 'Future pupil achievement'. Using Tunstall and Gipps' notion of 'achievement or improvement focused', a constituent element of giving feedback is target setting for pupils to help with achievement and improvement.

> *At its best [...] target setting is potentially and pre-eminently a means of helping us actually achieve what we aspire to, holding us to account to ourselves and others [...] it democratises achievement in the sense that it makes achievement possible for all and visible to all.* (Fielding, 1999)

Target setting for pupils is often done using the acronym 'SMART' – Specific, Measurable, Attainable, Relevant, Time-related. It is quite likely that you will have come across this before.

However, in the case of lessons involving an element of creativity, there is not necessarily a straightforward clear and linear progression through the process of creation to the end result. This can make SMART targets rather difficult to set, unless the teacher is in the position of knowing exactly what it is that the pupils are working on, and what the outcome is going to be.

REFLECTIVE TASK

Think about the pupils you considered in the Practical Task above and what targets you could set them. Are they SMART? Does it matter if they are not? Why? Why not?

Giving feedback in creative learning situations requires a degree of flexibility on the part of the teacher. It becomes important to 'think on your feet' and tailor feedback remarks to meet the specificity of the situation. This does not mean, however, that it is not possible to plan for them. Having a few questions ready when you begin dialogue with pupils will ease the way so you can begin to find out details regarding what is taking place in the creative tasks in your classroom.

Authenticity

Having considered some of the principal terminologies of assessment, we can now turn our attention to the sorts of tasks pupils can do which involve some aspect of creative learning. The dichotomy mentioned above between *creative processes* and *creative products* needs unpicking a little more from an assessment perspective. Earlier in this chapter the notion of 'authenticity' was introduced. An authentic task is one which is ... *representative of performance in the field* (Wiggins, 1989, p45), and therefore involves ... *the kind of activity that might require similar application of their knowledge, skills and understanding in the real, adult world* (James, 1998, p117). So an authentic task will involve coming up with a solution, or a set of solutions, to a problem which exists in the real world, and is not abstracted too far from reality. Examples of creative authentic tasks in various subject areas could include those listed below.

- *Maths*. How can a local newspaper increase the amount of text it gets onto a set page size?
- *Design and Technology*. The local primary school needs a new playground. What should it look like and what should it contain?
- *Geography*. How can clean water be supplied easily and cheaply to a village which the school has connections with in the third world?
- *History*. What sort of armour would have prevented Harold getting shot in the eye in 1066?
- *Biology*. How can hamsters be kept in more natural surroundings as pets?
- *Music*. A new product is being advertised on TV – what images should be used, and what music?
- *Maths/Design and Technology*. A fish pond is being built in a garden. What is the most suitable design for the space available?

PRACTICAL TASK PRACTICAL TASK PRACTICAL TASK PRACTICAL TASK PRACTICAL TASK

From the perspective of your specialist subject, think of two tasks which are authentic, and two which are not.

How these tasks will be organised depends on a number of factors. It may well be that teachers want their pupils to work in groups, and jointly try to come up with answers. This continues the notion of authenticity:

> *Many truly authentic tasks would be carried out by teams of workers. Simulating this team situation would provide opportunities for students to demonstrate skills of communication, co-operation and leadership.* (James, 1998, p119)

Process–product

Here the process–product dichotomy becomes something to which you will need to give some consideration. If the most important thing is the outcome, then you need not be overly concerned with *how* the pupils work and instead can concentrate solely on the ideas they produce. However, doing this negates the value of groups which may have worked really well together, come up with some truly creative solutions, yet been hampered by issues of implementation potentially beyond their control. This takes us into the domain of the third question asked at the outset of this chapter, 'why is it being assessed?' If the product is the thing that matters, then any form of assessment will be based on appropriateness, usability, and relevance. The notion of 'why' is contained in the product, the outcome. However, when the process of creative thinking, and of, say, fostering teamwork skills to work at a creative task, is the reason for doing a project, then it is the *process of doing* which is itself has become the focus. Dewey (1916) wrote of learning being *in* the doing, and this is what is going on here. When a creative task is being undertaken where learning lies in doing, then assessment needs to be focused onto the *activity*, onto what is going on, and for this we have already discussed how formative assessment is likely to be the most appropriate technique. We can now look in more detail at the final question that was asked at the outset of this chapter, 'what will be done with the assessment information?', and link this with 'why is it being assessed?'

PRACTICAL TASK PRACTICAL TASK **PRACTICAL TASK** PRACTICAL TASK **PRACTICAL TASK**

Next time you undertake any practical activity whatsoever in your classroom, consider whether it is the process of doing the task which is most important to *you* or the product which arises from it. Then consider the same thing from the perspectives of the pupils. Why not put it into 'pupil-speak' and ask them whether it was the *doing* or the *completion* (or whatever terms you wish to use – you know your classes!) which mattered most to them. Did their priorities match yours – if not, why?

Group work and social constructivism

Figure 5.2 showed how formative assessment of process happened while work was in progress. In situations of creative learning, teachers often choose to organise classes of pupils into groups, setting the groups working at tasks while circulating from one group to another, offering suggestions, giving feedback and ensuring that things run smoothly. This way of working is the result of a view of teaching and learning which employs a constructivist standpoint. In a constructivist view of learning the individual makes mental linkages between things they already know, their prior learning and new pieces of information or experiences. The process is one of construction of meaning for the individual. In the case of the group working at a creative task, this constructivism is situated in a social setting, the individual interacts with others and this helps build meaning from these interactions; an example of *social constructivism*.

Constructivism is a dominant paradigm in contemporary pedagogy, and it is appropriate to think about how views of learning affect the ways in which creative activities are undertaken in the classroom, as these get to the very heart of how we view and assess what is taking place.

RESEARCH SUMMARY RESEARCH SUMMARY **RESEARCH SUMMARY** RESEARCH SUMMARY

In a *behaviourist* view of learning, what is learned are behaviours. This view of learning comes from conditioning experiments with laboratory animals, the most famous example being Pavlov's work with dogs. In a behaviourist view little by way of mental operations are involved in creative processes. Indeed B.F. Skinner, one of the key figures in behaviourism, believed that the creative process was a result of stimulus–response interaction, and, as we have seen, the example he used was that of the poet, whose contribution to the poem he writes was not dissimilar to that of the chicken laying an egg (Perkins, 1988).

In a *transmission* view of education, the teacher has 'the knowledge' and the pupils are like empty vessels, waiting to have knowledge poured into them. These views present problems for us in terms of creativity. Behaviourist views of creativity do not have a high currency value these days and we can discount them fairly readily. But there is an important caveat here: creative *behaviours* are not the same thing as *behaviourism*. It is quite possible, indeed it is often desirable, to watch pupil actions as a part of formative assessment strategies in order to elicit data concerning their creative processes. As Craft observed:

> ... the observation and recording by the teacher of the behaviour of young children is particularly significant, as this highlights what is then novel for the individual child as meaning maker. (Craft, 2001, p24)

Constructivist views, on the other hand, do have something to offer. Important among constructivist views is Vygotsky's notion of the zone of proximal development (ZPD), wherein a child working with more able others is able to achieve at a higher level than they could unaided. This is a crucial notion for discussions of creativity and figures frequently in various sections throughout this book. However, constructivism is not the only way of viewing creativity in our classrooms. Indeed, as Perkins observes:

> ... complications make it important to deploy constructivist techniques wisely, in the right place for the right purpose. (Perkins, 1999)

Part of the fascination for pupils of undertaking creative tasks lies in the unexpected and the serendipitous – we are not asking them to construct meanings out of the obvious. In this case it does seem appropriate to think of cognitive connections being made, of instances of P-creativity (Boden, 1990), and of 'Eureka' moments.

This discussion of theory helps contextualise classroom creativity into learning paradigms. Schön (1983) talks of teachers 'espoused theories', ones which they hold, and 'theories in action', ones which they evidence. Atkinson and Claxton (2000) discuss how professionals are not always able to label exactly what it is that they are doing. To nurture and foster creativity in your classroom it is not essential to have a clear set of espoused theories, or to be able to label them, but it helps our discussion to see where some of the ideas we are examining originated from.

> **Teaching example – Key Stage 3 Science**
> In a science class the teacher wanted to deal with forces and motion. Instead of approaching this theoretically, she asked the class to discuss in small groups what they think would happen when different weights were swung on a piece of string. Discussing the task clarified the concepts for the pupils before they tried experimentation.

What is the connection between assessment, learning and creativity?

So, having looked at learning in our consideration of assessment, it is now logical to move to a consideration of the last of our questions from the beginning of the chapter.

> *Creativity and knowledge are not opposed to each other, even though an overemphasis on current knowledge can sometimes smother creativity. On the contrary, creative thinking cannot happen unless the thinker already possesses knowledge of a rich and/or well-structured kind.* (Boden, 2001, p95)

As we have seen, creative learning involves pupils forging new connections for themselves, building on prior knowledge, and then restructuring ideas in new and creative ways. The process of learning is not a linear one with all pupils moving in the same direction at the same time, and therefore formative assessment of what an individual should do for their next steps needs to be tailored for that specific pupil. Creative learning can also move in quite unexpected ways, and this too needs to be considered. In a linear approach to learning a wrong outcome is entirely feasible, yet how does that square with a view of teaching and learning which espouses creativity? If William Webb Ellis at Rugby School had not picked up a football and ran with it, the game of rugby would not have come into being. This was a divergent, unexpected act, 'wrong' in the rules of football, yet, it could be argued, it was also a creative one, in that a new game was created. Assessment processes for examples of divergent thinking need to be reflexive, and as a teacher you will need to use creative responses to respond appropriately. Linearity of teacher response is patently inappropriate when met with divergent pupil thinking.

Boundaries of appropriateness

However, there are occasions when divergent responses are not appropriate, and part of the role of assessment is to establish boundaries of appropriateness. For example, in a task brief which says 'design a dining table' the function and purpose of a dining table are fairly clearly defined – the use of the object is the reason it exists. A designer of a new dining table will take into account notions of flatness, of height, of heat-proof materials and of access. The resulting table is likely to be recognised by 'ordinary people'. Table design aficionados may discuss its aesthetics, and table design periodicals may feature it in articles, but it will be recognisable by its table-ness. Now, if an artist produces a piece called 'dining table' which features, say, a vertical surface covered in human body parts, 'ordinary people' would see this as a 'work of art' and would not try to serve their Sunday lunch on it. Art galleries might vie to exhibit it, and art cognoscenti may discuss the artist's statement that it represents the futility of quotidian existence during war-time, but its table-ness would be serving a non-utilitarian functionality. This distinction is important, because if the table designer for a furniture shop is asked for a new design and they come back with the vertical surface covered in body parts, they will have missed the essence of required table-ness which function, custom and practice have ascribed to such objects. So, in this case, this is a 'wrong' response. But is it always a 'wrong' response? The answer to this has to be 'no'. A creative response in an art lesson is different to a creative response in a design and technology lesson. How will assessment deal with this? Returning to Figure 5.2, we can see that formative assessment is taking place all the time that the pupils are working on the process of creation; it will be during these formative assessments, and during the feedback sessions, that issues of appropriateness will be dealt with. Figure 5.2 also shows us that future achievement arises influenced by formative assessment and target setting during the process stage, and so it is here too that decisions will be made which affect, and effect, what will come next.

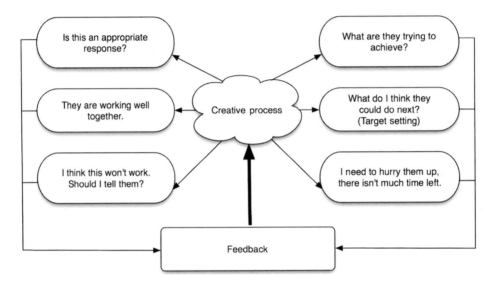

Fig. 5.3 Feedback

More on feedback

In the first task you were asked to think about feedback you could give to a group of pupils working at a task. We can revisit this now, and think about what sorts of areas feedback comments might address. In Figure 5.3 a series of possible feedback questions and comments are shown. The ways these feedback comments are framed will depend on the situation of your subject specialism and on the nature of the task being done.

REFLECTIVE TASK

How do the comments in Figure 5.3 relate to your response to the first task?

Connecting the strands

So far in this chapter we have dealt with a number of separate issues which impinge on the ways in which you can assess creative activities in the classroom. These topics include those listed below.

- **process–product**
- **formative assessment**
- **summative assessment**
- **feedback**
- **learning**
- **learning theory**
- **appropriateness**
- **authentic tasks.**

The final part of this chapter will pull together these disparate threads to show how you can use what you have found out when working with pupils in the classroom. A tacit but none-theless fundamental assumption of this chapter has been that creative learning, or teaching for creativity, engenders ways of working which are appropriate to be undertaken in all subject areas of the curriculum, and in cross-curricular learning too. It is the methodology of creative learning which is locatable in different contexts, which are assumed to be in normal schools, with normal conditions applying. In Figure 5.4 a diagrammatic representation of a creative task is shown, along with effectors and processes which we have discussed in this chapter. This shows the way in which you could deliver a task which involves a creative element in your lessons, the areas you need to consider, and how it needs to be located in a situation which acknowledges prior learning.

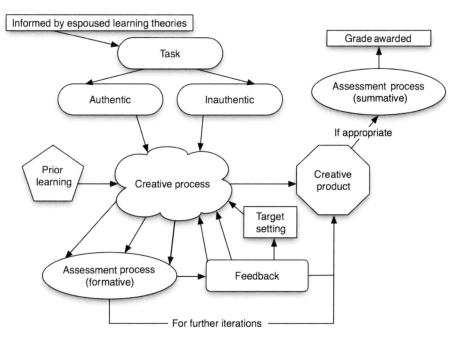

Fig. 5.4. Assessment of creative processes

Valuing the verbal

There have been, in the UK at least, a number of national initiatives aimed at improving classroom teaching and learning, looking at the role of formative assessment, principally the secondary (formerly Key Stage 3) strategy (DfES, 2004). However, despite these initiatives teachers sometimes still have concerns regarding the implementation of formative assessment. We know that some teachers do not consider their verbal comments made as feedback to be worthy of being considered as formative assessments, and that there is a perception that 'doing' assessment involves marking books. As one teacher asked:

> *Can I tell Ofsted that I'm making formative assessments every lesson, and for evidence they just need to watch me?* (Fautley, 2004)

We also know that:

> *Some teachers perceive that Ofsted inspections create a climate of fear. [...] They feel there are 'mixed messages' about assessment and that there is more pressure on summative assessment than support for formative assessment.* (Neesom, 2000, p6)

In opposition to this view, NACCCE (1999, p116) recommends that greater emphasis should be placed on formative assessment. It goes on to suggest that effective formative assessment should contain important principles:

- **It must be built into the design of the teaching programme as an integral element rather than added on to it.**
- **Pupils should be actively involved in the processes of assessment and contribute to them.**
- **It must be focused on the development of each individual, i.e. it must be criterion referenced rather than norm referenced.**
- **The evidence it provides must be acted on if teaching is to be tuned to the range of pupils' individual developments.**

(NACCCE, 1999, p131)

Managing and recording formative assessments

We have discussed the importance of formative assessment and of giving feedback, and we now need to consider ways in which you can manage this. If you are working with a number of classes over a series of lessons, then however high the quality, you will want to keep track of the feedback which has been given. Coping with this while you move between a number of groups working simultaneously can cause 'memory overload', and keeping track of progress over time can be an issue. Formative assessment is not always amenable to extensive documentation, but OFSTED (2003) noted that *In the best practice, teachers find effective ways to log this evidence of progress*. However, as we have seen, some teachers will be rightly concerned that an inspection regime may not recognise the verbal comments they make during the course of a lesson as being valid assessment material, but it is important that we recognise that it is. We have discussed the importance of verbal feedback being given with some immediacy, and how it involves a dialogue between teacher and pupils. Logging evidence of this is useful as both an *aide-mémoire*, and for charting the progress of an individual pupil. Having a simple class-list observation record which you fill in as you circulate between groups can go some way towards solving this. Here is an example from one such document, devised by a music teacher:

Name	Date	Unit of work	Notes	Date	Unit of work	Notes
Child A	xx/xx/xx	Patterns	Watched using glockenspiel, had some trouble with hitting notes	xx/xx/xx	Film music	Used Cubase, had really good idea for Section A of piece
Child B	xx/xx/xx	Blues	Provided a number of ideas for group piece	xx/xx/xx	Adverts	Had trouble editing piece

This sort of sheet can be readily adapted for use in any subject, and can be filled in as and when the occasion arises in a way which you find manageable and, most importantly, *useful*.

PRACTICAL TASK PRACTICAL TASK PRACTICAL TASK PRACTICAL TASK PRACTICAL TASK

We have asked a number of questions in this chapter, moving towards planning a creative task or activity, and thinking about the role that assessment – particularly formative assessment – will play in this. In order to do this a number of decisions need to be made, and the next task takes you through these sequentially. Working your way through it should give you sufficient information to plan a creative learning episode for one of your classes.

PRACTICAL TASK PRACTICAL TASK PRACTICAL TASK PRACTICAL TASK PRACTICAL TASK

What is the task you wish to undertake?

Why do you wish to do it?

>   What are the learning outcomes?

>   What is the task outcome?

Is it an authentic task?

>   If not (and there are many occasions when inauthentic tasks may be appropriate) do you have a different learning/task outcome in mind?

What prior learning do the pupils need to undertake this task?

>   Do they have it?

>   How do you know?

>   How, in turn, will this task become prior learning for something later in your syllabus?

Which is most important, the creative process, or the creative product?

>   Why?

How will you organise the class?

>   In groups – if so how? Friendship? Gender? Your own choice?

How long do you wish the task to last for?

>   During a lesson?

>   Less than a lesson?

>   As one of a number of such tasks within a unit of work?

>   More than a lesson?

What role will you adopt during the process?

>   Facilitator?

>   'Back seat'?

>   Critical friend?

How will you undertake formative assessment?

> As you circulate between groups?

> At specified times ('come and see me at 10 o'clock')?

How will you give feedback?

> There and then, verbally?

> In writing, later?

How will you set targets?

> Will these relate to process?

>> Ways of working?

>> Quality of ideas?

> Will these relate to product?

>> Fulfilling criteria?

>> Meeting specification or brief?

> Will they relate to task completion?

>> Getting the job done on time?

Will there be any summative assessment involved?

> If so, what are the criteria?

A SUMMARY OF **KEY POINTS**

In this chapter you have:

> considered the development of creative learning tasks;

> discussed how you can use formative assessment strategies to develop both creative responses *and learning* in your specialist subject;

> reflected on how formative assessment strategies can be built into tasks;

> practised what sorts of things are appropriate for you to say in feedback sessions;

> designed authentic tasks for your specialist subject;

> worked through planning a practical task for one of your classes.

The theme of formative assessment and AfL runs through this book like an *idée fixe*. It is, as many studies have observed, a key aspect of raising attainment.

FURTHER READING FURTHER READING **FURTHER READING** FURTHER READING

Airasian, P. (1991) *Classroom assessment*. New York: McGraw-Hill.

Assessment Reform Group (1999) *Assessment for learning – beyond the black box*. Cambridge: University of Cambridge School of Education.

Assessment Reform Group (2002) *Assessment for learning: 10 principles*. ARG. http://arg.educ. cam.ac.uk/CIE3.pdf

Black, P. (1993) Formative and summative assessment by teachers. *Studies in Science Education*, 21, 49–97.

Black, P. (1995) Can teachers use assessment to improve learning. *British Journal of Curriculum and Assessment*, 5 (2), 7–11.

Black, P., Harrison, C., Lee, C., Marshall, B. and Wiliam, D. (2003) *Assessment for learning: putting it into practice*. Maidenhead: Open University Press.

Cullingford, C. (1997) *Assessment versus evaluation*. London: Cassell.

DfES (2002) *Training materials for the Foundation subjects*. London: DfES.

DfES (2004) *Assessment for learning: guidance for senior leaders*. Norwich: HMSO.

Filer, A. (2000) *Assessment: social practice and social product*. London: RoutledgeFalmer.

McCallum, B. (2000) Formative assessment – implications for classroom practice.

Torrance, H. and Pryor, J. (1998) *Investigating formative assessment*. Buckingham: Open University Press.

Useful websites

www.aaia.org.uk   The Association for Achievement and Improvement through Assessment – some interesting documents.

http://arg.educ.cam.ac.uk/   Website for the Assessment Reform Group – influential thinkers on AfL.

www.ofsted.gov.uk/publications   OFSTED – look for documents on good assessment practice in your specialist subject.

www.standards.dfes.gov.uk/keystage3/   The Secondary Strategy – useful resources on AfL.

REFERENCES REFERENCES **REFERENCES** REFERENCES **REFERENCES** REFERENCES

Atkinson, T. and Claxton, G. (2000) *The intuitive practitioner: on the value of not always knowing what one is doing*. Buckingham: Open University Press.

Black, P. (1999) Assessment, learning theories and testing systems. In Murphy, P. (ed), *Learning and assessment*. London: Paul Chapman.

Black, P. and Wiliam, D. (1998) *Inside the black box: raising standards through classroom assessment*. London: School of Education, King's College.

Boden, M.A. (1990) *The creative mind: myths and mechanisms*. London: Weidenfeld & Nicolson.

Boden, M.A. (2001) Creativity and knowledge. In Craft, A., Jeffrey, B. and Leibling, M. (eds), *Creativity in education*. London: Continuum.

Craft, A. (2001) *An analysis of research and literature on creativity in education*. London: QCA.

Dewey, J. (1916) *Democracy and education*. New York: Free Press.

DfES (2004) *The Key Stage 3 strategy*. Online at: **www.standards.dfes.gov.uk/keystage3/**.

Fautley, M. (2004) Teacher intervention strategies in the composing processes of lower secondary school students. *International Journal of Music Education*, 22, 201–18.

Fielding, M. (1999) Targeting setting, policy pathology and student perspectives: learning to labour in new times. *Cambridge Journal of Education*, 29, 277–88.

Graue, M. (1993) Integrating theory and practice through instructional assessment. *Educational Assessment*, 1, 293–309.

James, M. (1998) *Using assessment for school improvement*. Oxford: Heinemann Educational.

McCallum, B. (2000) Formative assessment – implications for classroom practice. Available at: **www.qca.org.uk/download/formative(1).pdf** (accessed August 2006).

NACCCE (National Advisory Committee on Creative and Cultural Education) (1999) *All our futures: creativity, culture and education*. Sudbury, Suffolk: DfEE.

Neesom, A. (2000) *Report on teachers' perceptions of formative assessment*. London: QCA.

OFSTED (2003) *Good assessment practice in music*, HMI Document 1479. London: OFSTED.

Perkins, D. (1988) The possibility of invention. In Sternberg, R. (ed), *The nature of creativity*. Cambridge: Cambridge University Press.

Perkins, D (1999) The many faces of constructivism. *Educational Leadership*, 57, 6–11.

Schön, D. (1983) *The reflective practitioner*. Aldershot: Academic Publishing.

TGAT (1988) *Task group on assessment and testing: a report*. London: DES.

Torrance, E. Paul (1966) *Torrance tests of creative thinking: directions manual and scoring guide*. Lexington, MA: Personnel Press.

Tunstall, P. and Gipps, C. (1996) Teacher feedback to young children in formative assessment. *British Educational Research Journal*, 22, 389–405.

Wiggins, G. (1989) Teaching to the (authentic) test. *Educational Leadership*, 46, 41–7.

6

New technologies and creativity

By the end of this chapter you should understand:

- **how the development of your own skills with ICT relates to the award of QTS;**
- **what the role of ICT in the curriculum should be, both at a general and a subject level;**
- **how the educational use of ICT is situated within an educational context and how this can be investigated;**
- **how ICT facilitates teaching creatively, teaching for creativity and creative learning.**

This chapter will help you to meet the following Professional Standards for QTS:

Q17, Q23, Q25a

Introduction

The application of new technologies to support and develop teaching and learning has fundamentally altered the ways in which teachers and students are able to work. Bonnett describes the last ten years of the twentieth century as being a *seminal phase* in the history of government initiatives to consolidate and extend ICT in the curriculum (Bonnett et al., 1999, p345). Since then, the scope of the initiatives and the funding being made available (for hardware, software and teacher training) has been beyond any previous government's attempts at innovation (Somekh, 2000; Selwyn, 2002). The potential implications of these developments is that through the appropriate use of ICT your students are able to undertake authentic tasks that give rise to real outcomes, rather than hypothetical, non-realistic or pseudo-creative exercises that have no relevance to their own lives.

Ultimately, new technologies provide an opportunity for the development of creative approaches to teaching and learning. But this will make significant demands of you as a teacher in respect of subject content and pedagogy. This chapter explores some of these themes in the context of your initial teacher education. It considers:

- what types of skills you will need to acquire in order to make use of new technologies in your teaching;
- the context of ICT in the curriculum;
- the powerful mediating force that technology plays in shaping teaching and learning;
- how this analysis applies to our three themes of creative teaching, teaching for creativity and creative learning.

REFLECTIVE TASK
REFLECTIVE TASK

The increasing availability of hardware and software at reasonable prices has empowered teachers and students to work with ICT in ways which were unimaginable a few years ago.

This has had a huge impact on the content of the various curriculum areas and, with equal force, demanded that teachers reconsider their subject pedagogy as these new technologies become common teaching and learning tools.

Think about recent experiences in your own teaching practice. These could be related to observations you have done or lessons you have taught yourself. Have you seen:

- any examples of technologies being used in imaginative ways to inspire students' learning?
- lessons being taught which could not have been delivered without the use of a particular piece of ICT?
- examples of teachers developing their pedagogy as they bring old or new technologies into the classroom environment?
- what we might call creative teaching or learning inspired by or through the use of ICT in the classroom?

If you have the opportunity during a school placement, make some of these questions focus points for an observation of a lesson. Write up your reflection in a short paragraph.

Developing ICT skills and understanding for QTS

Meeting the government's standards for QTS is a vital part of your initial teacher education. Two main standards concern the use of ICT as part of teaching and learning. The supporting literature provided by the TDA illustrates what this standard might mean for you as a trainee teacher. The main messages are summarised below together with some application for our chapter theme.

Firstly, ICT has a legitimate and important role to play in most aspects of teachers' work in schools, e.g. in teaching and learning for individuals, small groups and whole classes, and in planning, assessment, evaluation, administration and management. There is range of software designed specifically to support these aspects of your work. As a trainee teacher you will have developed by the end of your course of study appropriate skills to support this overarching and supporting role for ICT. These skills will include the use of word processors, spreadsheets, databases and presentation software including interactive whiteboards. But these skills are not primarily about how ICT creatively informs and develops your teaching or your students' learning.

Secondly, you will need to develop the skill to know when it is appropriate to use ICT as part of your subject teaching and when to allow students to use it to help develop their learning. Part of this process involves considering the potential benefits of using ICT as a tool for teaching and learning. You will need to make informed decisions about the appropriateness of a piece of ICT as a way of facilitating teaching and learning on the basis of evidence drawn from their observations of other teachers, their own practice or their understanding of the subject literature related to this area. In this way, ICT becomes an important part of a teacher's pedagogy. Learning to be a good teacher with ICT is not just about knowing how to use the technology itself. It is about learning to use it appropriately, at the right time and for the right purpose. So what is the role of ICT in the curriculum? And what are you, as a trainee teacher, expected to do with it?

ICT in the secondary curriculum

The role of ICT in the secondary curriculum has been clearly laid out in recent government publications. For example, at Key Stage 3 students will need to be:

- *taught the programme of study, at each key stage, as set out in the National Curriculum for Information and Communication Technology – the attainment target, ICT capability, sets out the expected standard of students' performance required at each level;*
- *given opportunities to apply and develop their ICT capability through the use of ICT tools to support their learning in all subjects.*

(DfES, 2004, p9)

In addition, at Key Stage 4 students should be given opportunities to:

1. *Apply and develop their ICT capability through the use of ICT tools to support their learning in all subjects;*
2. *Support their work by being taught to:*
- *find things out from a variety of sources, selecting and synthesising the information to meet their needs and developing an ability to question its accuracy, bias and plausibility;*
- *develop their ideas using ICT tools to amend and refine their work and enhance its quality and accuracy;*
- *exchange and share information, both directly and through electronic media;*
- *review, modify and evaluate their work, reflecting critically on its quality, as it progresses.*

(www.nc.uk.net/nc_resources/html/about_NC.shtml)

Put simply, ICT should be taught as an independent subject during Key Stages 3 and 4. In addition, all subjects have to make use of ICT to support teaching and learning. However:

The effective balance between the teaching of ICT skills, knowledge and under-standing on the one hand and the application of these as part of learning across subjects on the other hand remains a difficult and elusive goal for the majority of schools. (OFSTED, 2002/03, p10)

Research done during the ImpaCT2 project (DfES, 2002) reflected on this issue. A key finding from this report stated that:

For many schools the main focus of activity following installation of networked ICT infrastructure was on teaching ICT skills. Cross-curricular use of ICT is difficult for secondary schools to achieve because ICT has traditionally been a specialist subject for GCSE. A major shift in culture and established practice is involved in the introduction of ICT within subject teaching. (DfES, 2002, p19; my emphasis)

The use of ICT as a tool for creativity in education requires a fundamental and detailed look at aspects of an individual teacher's pedagogy. But it also requires teachers to have a broader view of what their 'subject' entails. As we have seen the QCA's consultation on the curriculum (QCA, 2005a) has many relevant points here. Not least is the challenge to explore and utilise the potential of new technologies for individual subject areas:

In a technology-rich world we need to review and modernise what and how we learn. Imagine how a graphic designer works today compared with 30 years ago. What should a modernised music, art or design curriculum be like? ... They may use technology as a tool for thinking, making or doing. (QCA, 2005a)

Figure 6.1 illustrates the process of applying ICT in your teaching as a tool to facilitate teaching creatively, teaching for creativity and creative learning. It is important to remember that although we considered each of these three themes in separate chapters in the early part of this book, as you develop your teaching skills through your ongoing experiences, you should develop a sense that they are all part of a unified approach to teaching. This approach will affect everything you do as a teacher. As we saw in the previous chapter, how you assess your pupils will alter dramatically; in this chapter, the commitment to use ICT as a tool to promote creativity in your classrooms will have some important consequences in what your pupils will learn, how they learn it and, of course, your own pedagogy.

PRACTICAL TASK PRACTICAL TASK **PRACTICAL TASK** PRACTICAL TASK **PRACTICAL TASK**

Each subject within the National Curriculum at Key Stage 3 has to make use of ICT. There is a range of online materials devoted to exemplifying approaches to teaching and learning with ICT or giving general guidance about areas to develop further. These include:

- the National Curriculum Online (*www.nc.uk.net/*)
- the National Curriculum in Action site (*www.ncaction.org.uk/*)
- OFSTED subject reports for 2004/05 (*www.ofsted.gov.uk/publications/annualreport0405/*)

Each of these sites will give you a broad overview of how you might be expected to use ICT in your teaching. As you look at your particular subject area in more detail, ask yourself the following questions:

- How might the use of ICT in this subject area inspire creative responses from my students?
- How does my subject curriculum facilitate my being able to teach creatively using ICT as a tool for teaching for creativity?
- Will these approaches to ICT allow me to support my students' creative learning?

Finally, summarise in a short paragraph your view on the opportunities that your subject affords for the use of ICT as a teaching and learning tool.

Having examined how ICT should be used in theory, we will move on to explore the way in which ICT intervenes in the processes of teaching and learning through Wertsch's notion of 'mediated action' (Wertsch, 1998, p25).

ICT and mediated action

A basic understanding of Wertsch's work is very helpful in considering how ICT might move beyond the supporting of a static, functional delivery of knowledge towards facilitating teaching creatively, teaching for creativity and creative learning. His notion of mediated action allows us to consider relationships between teachers, learners and pieces of technology. Wertsch views pieces of technology as being interactive within the context in which they are introduced and used. In education, the mediating properties of technology influence:

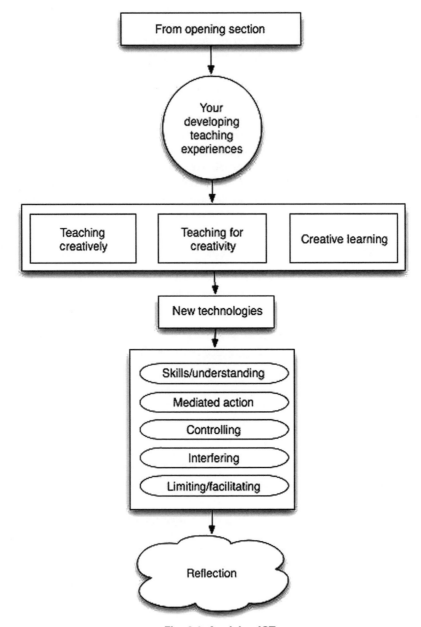

Fig. 6.1. Applying ICT

- **the learning environment of the classroom;**
- **the nature of the curriculum subjects;**
- **the understanding of teachers and students.**

One of the keys to truly engaging with the potential creative power of ICT is to recognise that ICT mediates teaching and learning processes between these three groups. Within these interactions there may be tensions because *mediated action is often organised around multiple, and often conflicting, goals* (Wertsch, 1998, p34). In other words, ICT has the potential to transform teaching and learning in each subject area providing that you and your students are open-minded to the new possibilities and actively engaged in exploring their potential. If not, there might be a disjuncture between what you or your students expect or want a piece of technology to do and the technology's inherent potential. By documenting and analysing this mediated action it is possible to view the relationship between you, your students and the particular piece of technology. These ideas have a rich application for you as a trainee teacher as you reflect on classroom events and develop your teaching skills.

But Wertsch also notes a spin-off effect when one considers the effect of mediated action within a social environment such as a classroom (Wertsch, 1998, p53). A student or teacher's original intentions or goals may lose or change their meaning with the introduction of the piece of technology. Since technologies are being continuously changed and interpreted by teachers and students their original purpose or intent can undergo many revisions. Wertsch characterises this feature of mediated action in terms of 'appropriation' or 'resistance' (Wertsch, 1998, p56). It is possible for you and your students to 'interpret', 'appropriate' or 'resist' ICT through a process of mediated action in such a way that facilitates or limits teaching and learning opportunities.

PRACTICAL TASK PRACTICAL TASK PRACTICAL TASK PRACTICAL TASK PRACTICAL TASK

Review your responses to the previous task.

Compare the ways in which you might seek to learn about how a new piece of technology works as an independent learner with the approaches that you have seen in similar periods of instruction during your classroom observations. Imagine you have been given a new digital camera.

- What is the first thing you do with it once it is out of the box?

- Where do you go with it?

- If you get stuck with how to use it, where or from whom would you seek to get help?

- What supporting technologies do you use with it? How do you organise these as you seek to develop your skills with the new camera?

- How do you balance the activities related to 'learning how to use it' with the 'learning what I could achieve with it'?

- Do you feel comfortable learning by trial and error or would you rather be led through the potential of the camera by an experienced user or a manufacturer's guide?

Think about how you would develop the skills of using your new digital camera for a particular purpose, e.g. taking a series of photographs of a friend's wedding.

- What about the skills that you need that go beyond those associated with operating the digital camera itself?

- Where do these skills come from and how did you/do you develop them?

- How does the digital camera itself facilitate or limit the process of taking this series of photographs?

- How would you describe the 'mediating properties' of your new digital camera? How has it affected your skills as a photographer, what you have learnt and how you achieved the task of documenting your friend's wedding?

ICT as a creative opportunity for teaching and learning

Within the existing network of relationships between a teacher, the student and the classroom environment, ICT exerts its influence on teaching and learning. The principles of mediated action allow us to explore this further. What forms might these influences take? Drawing on a series of three musical metaphors, we will consider how ICT has the potential to control, interfere with, facilitate or limit processes of teaching creatively and teaching for creativity.

Controlling technologies?

All technologies exercise forms of control over their users. These can be positive and enabling or negative and limiting. In practice it means that technologies can extend or limit the potential for effective teaching or learning. For example, work done by Folkestad, Hargreaves and Lindström (1998) identified that a piece of software that allowed students to record sounds on different instruments within different tracks of sound clearly initiated or predicated a particular way of working ('vertical' musical composition) on students. To work in a contrasting way ('horizontally') required a considerable amount of devious effort on the part of the student but was something that some teachers felt worth encouraging.

Interfering technologies?

Theodor Adorno, the famous twentieth-century musicologist, once commented that:

> There is a requirement for an approach to the design of hardware and software for musical applications to which the key is flexibility of interaction. The composer should be empowered to realise the fruits of his or her artistic imagination without the 'interposition of the equipment' being 'stamped on every tone'. (Adorno, 1954, p110)

ICT can interfere with learning in a number of ways. Students may be unable to complete a learning task because the technology is literally interfering with their ability to work, perhaps by being overtly complex or difficult to understand. But the opposite might be the case. A software environment might be extremely empowering in one sense but very limited in others. It might unhelpfully restrict the amount of personal application or input that a student can make of it, resulting in pieces of work that are so similar and bland as to be little help in allowing students to develop their knowledge, skill or understanding. You will need to make very careful choices about the types of hardware and software that support teaching and learning in your subject and be very alert to the possibility of ICT interfering in students' learning in an unhelpful way.

Limiting or facilitating technologies?

> Working with piano sounds makes me pay closer attention to the real structure of the song. It strips the song down to the most plain kind of version. (Laurie Anderson, in Théberge, 1997, pp198–9)

In the final part of our musical metaphor, the American musician and performance artist Laurie Anderson expresses her preference when writing songs for limiting the number of sounds she has available at any one time. Working at the piano, rather than in her recording studio with an abundance of musical instruments, allows her to pay attention to the 'real structure' of the song. This is an interesting metaphor for teaching with ICT. We might suppose that a technologically rich teaching and learning environment would present the best and most facilitating environment for creativity, but here we have an artist who is deliberately restricting choices in favour of a simpler model of expression. As a teacher, you will have to make choices about when and when not to use ICT. Remember that on occasions the limiting potential of a piece of technology may be exactly what is required for a student to learn a particular lesson or come to understand a new concept. A key for truly creative teaching and learning may be to deliberately reduce the use of ICT in the teaching environment for a specific purpose and a specific length of time.

While acknowledging that ICT may control, interfere with and limit teaching and learning within the classroom context, it is important to recognise that there are many other applications of ICT that will inspire and facilitate creativity in your teaching.

ICT and teaching creatively

As examined in Chapter 2, the NACCCE report described teaching creatively as:

Teachers using imaginative approaches to make learning more interesting, exciting and effective. (NACCCE, 1999, p6)

Craft (2005, p42) summarises approaches to teaching creatively as:

- **using imaginative approaches;**
- **making learning more interesting;**
- **being effective.**

Teaching creatively involves an active decision, made by you, to do things in a way that will seize the attention of the students. Many teachers have interpreted this to mean that only bizarre or 'wacky' ways of working fit this category. While this may well be the case, as we have seen in Chapter 2 more measured responses also fall into this approach. Teachers involved in active learning or activity-based learning may well be teaching creatively. Teachers who bring real-world examples for problem-solving, or who set up discussion groups, or who consider the social component of learning in class may also be teaching creatively. The essence of this approach is that it treats the student as an active participant in their learning.

ICT can empower approaches to teaching creatively providing that your decisions to use particular pieces of ICT are well considered and relate to wider pedagogical concerns that you have identified. ICT is only a tool and is not the sole answer to inspiring and capturing imaginations. The novelty of using an interactive whiteboard in the classroom, or a new set of digital art tools, or students exploring geography through Google Earth, will only last a short time. Students will quickly want to see and understand how new technologies facilitate their learning of new ideas and develop their understandings in a particular subject. As a trainee teacher, it is vital that you consider how the general teaching skills of effective planning, classroom management, lesson pace and adopting a range of assessment strategies develop alongside your introduction of new technologies.

ICT and teaching for creativity

As we have seen in Chapter 3, teaching for creativity entails:

Teachers developing young people's own creative thinking or behaviour, and includes teaching creatively. (NACCCE, 1999, p6)

Teaching creatively and teaching for creativity are closely linked, but teaching for creativity entails taking the students on a creative journey where their responses are not predetermined. Teaching for creativity means that the students will be producing ideas that may well involve novelty and, possibly, experimentation. Teachers and students involved in teaching for creativity will be engaged with processes, and although products may well be important, it is in the process of creation where the true focus lies.

Craft (2005, p42) identifies that teaching for creativity involves:

- **the passing of control to the learner and the encouraging of innovative contributions;**
- **teachers placing a value on learners' ownership and control, when innovation often follows;**
- **encouraging students to pose questions, identify problems and issues;**
- **offering students the opportunity to debate and discuss their thinking;**
- **encouraging children to be co-participant in learning, resulting in further control for learners over appropriate strategies for their learning;**
- **being at the least learner considerate and ideally 'learner inclusive', thus prioritising learner 'agency';**
- **encouraging 'creative learning', the construction of 'creative learners' and ultimately the 'creative individual'.**

Again, new technologies can help in all these areas but they are not the sole answer. They can allow for a greater sense of independent learning within carefully constructed environments. Within these learning contexts, your students can be truly innovative, experimental and creative and grapple with creative processes of learning. Similarly, students can engage in a greater sense of collaboration and communication both within and beyond classrooms through ICT. Innovative approaches to shared learning environments allow students the chance to ask questions, discuss issues and debate alternative solutions with an increasing sense of confidence.

Finally, an approach to teaching for creativity with ICT acknowledges that ICT may, in some cases, fundamentally alter the nature of the tasks that you set for your students. For example, Sound2Game (UCan.tv, 2005) allows students to take on the role of sound designer for a computer game. Within the software, students have to design sounds for five computer game scenarios, matching sounds to particular actions and environments through a systematic process of trial and experimentation. This is something that was impossible to do before computers had enough processing power to structure and manipulate sounds in a digital format. Similarly, the potential of Google Earth as a software learning environment has huge potential for the teaching of geography; something picked up on recently in Wolverhampton's City Learning Centre (Wolverhampton CLC, 2006).

ICT extends and enriches traditional curriculum subjects with new skills, understanding and knowledge. While you will maintain overall control of what students are working through in a given lesson, and will have set appropriate learning objectives to that end, the truly creative use of ICT in your classroom will allow students the chance to follow through divergent pathways of learning towards these ends. In this sense, your students can learn with or through the technology. You will need to be aware of these alternative pathways through subject content and should attempt to document them and engage students in them using principles drawn from assessment for learning strategies.

ICT and creative learning

As we have seen in Chapter 4, creative learning is a term that has multiple meanings. We have discussed how creative learning can occur when teachers teach creatively to foster creativity. Creative learning is active and often experiential. Although it could be considered that all learning is creative, in that new cognitive connections are made where previously none existed, creative learning engages the student with creative processes, creative outcomes, or creative thinking.

The QCA (2005b, 2005c) outlines five areas of students' learning that provide evidence of creative learning taking place.

1. **Questioning and challenging.**
2. **Making connections, seeing relationships.**
3. **Envisaging what might be.**
4. **Exploring ideas, keeping options open.**
5. **Reflecting critically on ideas, actions, outcomes.**

The 'Identifying Creativity in the Curriculum' photography project in Sheffield (High Storrs, 2005) investigated students' perceptions of creative learning. While students learnt the basic skills required to use a digital camera skilfully, they also reflected on their learning process and began to see how creative learning worked. The final report from the project commented that:

> *Most creative lessons were when students were being taught creatively and where teachers took account of different learning styles and varied tasks throughout the lessons. When the students were creative we found that they discussed ideas, put ideas forward, argued their points, worked alone and collaboratively, accessed help and guidance from the creative practitioner and teacher throughout the process, took risks and developed their insight into creative learning. It became very clear that creativity and skills acquisition complemented each other.* (High Storrs, 2005, p2)

It will be no surprise that these outcomes can be facilitated through the use of ICT as a teaching and learning tool but they are dependent on you making appropriate choices, firstly related to how you structure subject content and secondly about which pieces of ICT you decide to use. These things will not happen automatically. They require careful planning. But there is overwhelming evidence from a number of projects (Savage and Challis, 2002; Jeffrey, 2004; Murphy et al., 2004; QCA, 2005b, 2005c) that ICT can be used in a number of ways to stimulate and develop students' creative learning. Finally, in the High Storrs project it was interesting to note that researchers found a clear link between students' acquisition of skills related to photography and their ability to engage in creative learning.

PRACTICAL TASK PRACTICAL TASK **PRACTICAL TASK** PRACTICAL TASK **PRACTICAL TASK**

Analyse a lesson that you have taught that involved you or your students using a piece of hardware of software. Consider the following questions:

- How did the piece of ICT control, interfere with, limit or facilitate the students' learning?
- How did the piece of ICT allow you to teach creatively or teach for creativity?
- How did the piece of ICT allow your students to engage in creative learning processes?
- How do you know that the ICT facilitated creativity in respect of teaching and learning during that lesson? Were you able to document this evidence and talk about it during your analysis and evaluation? What would be the best way of sharing this information with other teachers?

Conclusion

Where or when does the truly creative use of ICT occur? Interestingly, OFSTED seems to think that this occurs more often in students' use of technology in informal learning contexts such as the home:

> *Tasks incorporating the use of ICT are often over-structured – both in ICT lessons and more widely. This is somewhat ironic because ICT can be very effective at motivating students to learn and to take this learning forward on their own. Independent learning is characterised by tenacity and self-motivation on the part of the learner; the personalised nature of learning with ICT lends itself well to promoting this. Examples of this are still relatively rare in schools, although more prevalent in students' use of computers at home, often in gaming situations.*
> (OFSTED, 2005)

The potential of ICT to allow for independent learning and the personalisation of subject knowledge is a key characteristic of creative learning and a key aim of teaching for creativity. It is a sobering thought that we could be limiting the creative potential of new technologies through inappropriate pedagogical application of a potentially liberating resource. OFSTED has identified a tendency for teachers to overstructure tasks within classrooms. Perhaps this is understandable, but as a trainee teachers you should be encouraged to be innovative and creative in this area. Things do not have to be taught in the way they have always been. There is an opportunity here for truly creative teaching and learning practices that should be seized by all.

A SUMMARY OF **KEY POINTS**

> ICT can support and develop teaching and learning.
> Your personal skills with ICT are very important, but knowing when or when not to use ICT with your students is a vital decision.
> ICT mediates the teaching and learning processes between teachers, students and the wider educational environment.
> Teaching creatively with ICT must be related to the wider pedagogical framework of your teaching.

> Teaching for creativity with ICT involves giving a greater degree of ownership of the learning process to your students and will fundamentally affect the structure of your teaching activities.

> ICT can facilitate the process of creative learning if your definitions of subject content are broad enough and you are prepared to give students the learning 'spaces' require to explore ideas and keep their options open.

FURTHER READING   FURTHER READING   **FURTHER READING**   FURTHER READING

Sefton-Green, J. (ed) (1999) *Young people, creativity and new technologies: the challenge of the digital arts*. London: Routledge.

Selwyn, N. (2002) *Telling tales on technology: qualitative studies of technology and education*. Aldershot: Ashgate.

Somekh, B. and Davis, N. (eds) (1997) *Using information technology effectively in teaching and learning: studies in pre-service and in-service teacher education*. London: Routledge.

Useful websites

DfES, *Key Stage 3 National Strategy: ICT across the curriculum*. Online at: **www.standards.dfes.gov.uk/keystage3/respub/ictac** (accessed 10 February 2006).

NESTA Futurelab (2006) *Literature review in creativity, new technologies and learning: a report for NESTA Futurelab*. Online at: **www.nestafuturelab.org/research/reviews/cr01.htm** (accessed 10 February 2006).

OFSTED, *ICT in secondary schools: the annual report of HMCI for schools 2004/05*. Online at: **www.ofsted.gov.uk/publications/annualreport0405/4.2.8.html**

QCA, *Creativity: find it, promote it!* Online at: **www.ncaction.org.uk/creativity/about.htm**

REFERENCES   REFERENCES   **REFERENCES**   REFERENCES   **REFERENCES**   REFERENCES

Adorno, T. (1954) The ageing of the new music. *Telos*, 77, 95–116.

Bonnett, M., McFarlane, A. and Williams, J. (1999) ICT training in subject teaching: an opportunity for curriculum renewal. *Curriculum Journal*, 10 (3), 345–59.

Craft, A. (2005) *Creativity in schools: tensions and dilemmas*. London: Routledge.

DfES (2002) *Students' and teachers' perceptions of ICT in the home, school and community*. London: DfES.

DfES (2004) *Key Stage 3 National Strategy: ICT across the curriculum (management guide)*. London: DfES. Online at: **www.standards.dfes.gov.uk/keystage3/respub/ictac** (accessed 10 February 2006).

High Storrs (2005) *Identifying creativity in the curriculum: a photography project at High Storrs School, Sheffield*. Online at: **www.creative-partnerships.com/projects/95752/** (accessed 10 February 2006).

Jeffrey, B. (2004) *End of award report: creative learning and student perspectives (CLASP) project*, submitted to ESRC, November.

Murphy, P., McCormick, B., Lunn, S., Davidson, M. and Jones, H. (2004) *Electronics in schools, final evaluation report, executive summary*. London/Milton Keynes: DTI/OU.

NACCCE (1999) *All our futures: creativity, culture and education*. Sudbury, Suffolk: DfEE.

OFSTED (2002/03) *Ofsted subject reports 2002/03: information and communication technology in secondary schools*. London: OFSTED. Online at: **www.ofsted.gov.uk/publications/index.cfm?fuseaction=pubs.summary&id=3540** (accessed 10 February 2006).

OFSTED (2005) *ICT in secondary schools: the annual report of HMCI for Schools 2004/05*. Online at: **www.ofsted.gov.uk/publications/annualreport0405/4.2.8.html** (accessed 10 February 2006).

QCA (2005a) *Futures: meeting the challenge* (Forces for change, point 2). Online at: **www.qca.org.uk** (accessed 1 February 2005).

QCA (2005b) *Creativity: find it, promote it! Promoting students' creative thinking and behaviour across the curriculum at Key Stages 1 and 2* (video pack). London: QCA.

QCA (2005c) *Creativity: find it, promote it! Online at:* **www.ncaction.org.uk/creativity/about.htm** (accessed 10 February 2006).

Savage, J. and Challis, M. (2002) A digital arts curriculum? Practical ways forward. *Music Education Research*, 4 (1), 7–24.

Selwyn, N. (2002) *Telling tales on technology: qualitative studies of technology and education*. Aldershot: Ashgate.

Somekh, B. (2000) New technology and learning: policy and practice in the UK, 1980–2010. *Education and Information Technologies*, 5 (1), 19–37.

Théberge, P. (1997) *Any sound you can imagine: making music/consuming technology*. London: Wesleyan University Press.

UCan.tv (2005) Sound2Game. Online at: **www.sound2game.net** (accessed 23 March 2006).

Vygotsky L. (1978) *Mind in society: the development of higher psychological processes*. Cambridge, MA: Harvard University Press.

Wertsch, J. (1998) *Mind as action*. New York and Oxford: Oxford University Press.

Wolverhampton CLC (2006) **http://blog.wolverhamptonclc.co.uk/2006/02/05/google-earth-in-education/** (accessed 23 March 2006).

7
Creativity and inclusion

By the end of this chapter you should:

- **have a clear understanding of what is meant by inclusion and how creative approaches to teaching and learning can create an inclusive educational environment;**
- **distinguish between different types of creative outcomes and processes which demonstrate that all students can be creative in varying degrees;**
- **be able to think through how generic creative attributes apply within your own subject area and formulate approaches to teaching and learning that encourage their development.**

This chapter will help you to meet the following Professional Standards for QTS:

Q1, Q2, Q7, Q10, Q19

Introduction

Creativity is for all! It is vital that we state this clearly and unambiguously at the beginning of this important chapter. As we have seen in the previous chapters, creativity can become an important feature of our work as teachers and of our students' work too given our clear example and lead. Creativity should permeate through all levels of our work as teachers, informing our planning, interactions with students, designing of lesson tasks and activities, our assessment processes and use of resources such as ICT.

So, in one sense, there is no doubt that creativity should be firmly established within an effective model of teaching and learning that encompasses teaching creatively, teaching for creativity and creative learning. But is it really realistic to expect all students to be creative? Aren't some students going to be more creative than others? And how can a busy classroom teacher really spot creativity and nurture it on an individual, case-by-case, basis? If all students can be creative, what are the skills, knowledge and understanding that they should be developing?

REFLECTIVE TASK

Our supposition that creativity is for all logically leads to an emphasis on inclusion where all students can succeed, to a greater or lesser extent, at being creative. Take a few moments to reconsider the definition of creativity we presented in Chapter 1. Think through the implications of this definition for your teaching through the following questions:

- What are the specific creative outcomes or processes that you are hoping your students might develop?
- Is it possible to define, in advance, the particular creative skills, knowledge and understanding that students will obtain during a sequence of lessons?
- What might an inclusive approach to creativity look like in your subject? How do you think you could judge one student's creative output against another?

Creativity for all

Before we go on to look at some of the issues relating to educational inclusion and how these relate to our central thesis of creativity as a key to effective teaching and learning, it is important to place our hypothesis of creativity being for all students on a firmer footing. We will do this through a brief analysis of two main theories that we discussed in our opening chapter: Craft's 'little c creativity' and Boden's 'P- and H-creative' categories. These two theories will be central to the practical application of teaching creatively, teaching for creativity and creative learning as you teach inclusively. Figure 7.1 shows the main flow of thought that underpins this chapter in relation to our principal themes.

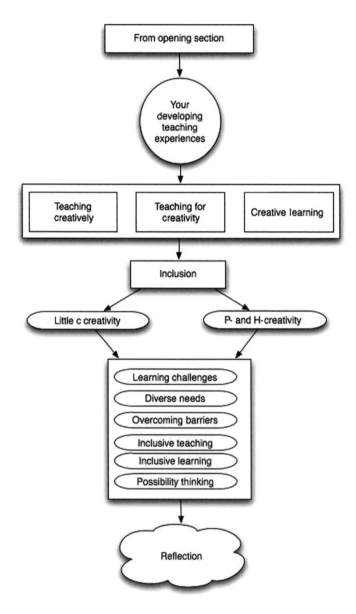

Fig. 7.1. Chapter 7: overview

Craft's little c creativity

Craft's notion of little c creativity is well established (Craft, Jeffrey and Leibling, 2001, p45). Little c creativity is contrasted with high creativity, by which she means *the extraordinary creativity of the genius in any particular field* (ibid., p46). High creativity has certain characteristics such as innovation, novelty and excellence and may break with past understandings or perspectives. High creativity can actually change or refashion knowledge domains. By definition, high creativity is only achieved by a very few people who make an extraordinary impact in their field.

Little c creativity, by contrast, is defined as being *an approach to life which is driven to find solutions and ways through all situations, an approach to life which assumes a 'can do' attitude* (ibid., p49). It is something that all us can develop and is, fundamentally, shaped by our life experiences and the various social and cultural contexts we interact with including, most importantly, our educational institutions.

How can one spot little c creativity? Craft distinguishes various criteria that can separate one's behaviour as being little c creative or not. Little c creativity:

- *involves the active and intentional taking of action in the world;*
- *is a way of coping with everyday challenges, which may involve knowledge-based intuition just as much as step-by-step thought;*
- *involves innovation;*
- *involves a 'moving on';*
- *may involve problem identification as well as problem-solving.*

Boden's P- and H-creative categories

Creativity draws crucially on our ordinary abilities. Noticing, remembering, seeing, speaking, hearing, understanding language, and recognizing analogies: all these talents of Everyman are important. (Boden, 1990, p261)

Alongside Craft's notion of little c creativity, Boden also considers a certain type of creativity to be based in the everyday and familiar. Craft refers to this type of creativity as possessing the components of a 'way of life' (Craft, Jeffrey and Leibling, 2001, pp45, 56); Boden relates creativity to the 'ordinary abilities' that the majority of us possess and can learn to utilise in a creative way.

More specifically, as we saw briefly in Chapter 1, Boden's work is helpful in allowing us to draw distinctions about the type of creative work that a student may produce in response to a particular activity (Boden, 1990). How do you know if a students' work is original and valuable? How do you know if it is creative, or whether the process by which it was 'created' has been characterised by creative elements? Within the classroom, Boden suggests that it is worthwhile to consider the difference between work that is deemed to be original to the producer and work that is original in wider terms. The distinction is between work that is original to the person producing it and work that is original to society as a whole. Acts of creativity which can be termed psychological, in the sense of having occurred to an individual, are categorised as being P-creative; those which, although coming into being in the same fashion, also have a historical importance beyond that of the immediate individual are designated as H-creative:

> *... a P-creative idea need not be unusual. It is a novelty for the person generating it, but not necessarily for anyone else. We may even be able to predict that the person concerned will have that P-creative idea in the near future, yet its being predictable does not make it any less creative. Indeed ... every human infant is creative. For children's minds develop not just by learning new facts, and not just by playfully combining them in novel ways, but also by coming to have ideas which they simply could not have had before.* (Boden, 1990, p48)

Craft's notion of little c creativity and Boden's distinctions between P- and H-creative are both helpful as a background for our investigation of creativity and inclusion. If, as we have stated, creativity is something that we should expect and encourage all students to develop, we need to understand precisely what the process of creativity might look like and what its end products might contain and mean for individual students. The redefining of creativity in education through little c creativity theory and P-creative work means that all students, regardless of academic ability, can have the potential to be creative and develop creative skills. Boden's work also suggests that, importantly, teachers might also be able to predict when P-creative work might occur for individual pupils in their classrooms. Creativity is, by these definitions, inclusive. A creative approach to teaching and learning can lead to a more inclusive educational environment that will benefit all students.

PRACTICAL TASK PRACTICAL TASK **PRACTICAL TASK** PRACTICAL TASK **PRACTICAL TASK**

Spend some time considering your own subject discipline, in particular:

- **analyse the important creative processes and outcomes that have shaped its history;**
- **reflect on your own engagement with the subject over recent years and highlight any moments when you have adopted creative processes or produced creative outcomes that were personally significant or meaningful;**
- **consider any concepts, theories or practices that you found hard to learn through traditional methods of teaching or learning.**

For each of the above points, translate your own experiences into the context of your own teaching. Ask yourself the following questions:

- **How can 'authentic' creative processes and outcomes in your subject be introduced, represented or taught in a way that all students in your classroom will understand?**
- **Through your teaching, how can you make your subject personally meaningful and significant to your students? How can creative processes or products assist you in this task?**
- **How can a creative approach to teaching and learning allow you to broaden the opportunities for students to work through concepts, theories or practices that may be difficult to teach in traditional ways?**

Creativity and the inclusion agenda

Educational inclusion is at the heart of the National Curriculum at Key Stage 3 and its principles and practices also extend into Key Stages 4 and 5. Within each of the core subjects within the National Curriculum there are statements related to inclusion and important principles to which teachers are required, by law, to have due regard. One of the key messages of this book has been that curriculum documentation, GCSE specification and other government publications should not stifle creative approaches to teaching and learning. Rather, they can be interpreted through the 'lens' of your own, individual teaching style.

That said, it is important to understand, appreciate and follow through key curriculum themes from national legislation in your teaching practice. Inclusion has been one of these very important themes that has focused the minds of some of the best educational thinkers over the last ten years. A summary of the thinking behind the National Curriculum documentation on inclusion is provided below. Similar themes can be seen in specifications drawn from Key Stages 4 and 5. It is important to reinforce our knowledge of this before moving onto a consideration of how it relates to creativity.

Within the National Curriculum, three main principles for inclusion have been identified.

1. Setting suitable learning challenges.
2. Responding to students' diverse learning needs.
3. Overcoming potential barriers to learning and assessment for individuals and groups of students.

Setting suitable learning challenges

Every student needs to have the opportunity to experience success in learning and achieve as high a standard as possible. While curriculum materials contain suggestions about curriculum content, how this content is delivered remains, largely, within the professional judgement of the individual teacher (although this does vary on a subject-by-subject basis). It is important that differentiation is used effectively to target the content of a programme of study to the requirements of individual students, e.g. by extending the breadth and depth of study within a subject or, interestingly, by drawing on the content of different subjects.

Responding to students' diverse learning needs

All students should be set high expectations and given opportunities to succeed. Teachers need to be aware of the different experiences, interests and strengths that students bring with them into the school and use these to plan appropriately to ensure students' full engagement during lessons. Teachers need to be aware of equal opportunities legislation that covers race, gender and disability. In a useful summary, the curriculum documentation demonstrates how teachers should take specific action to respond to students' diverse needs by:

- **creating effective learning environments;**
- **securing their motivation and concentration;**
- **providing equality of opportunity through teaching approaches;**
- **using appropriate assessment approaches;**
- **setting targets for learning.**

Overcoming potential barriers

Within this section the curriculum documentation makes the general point that all teachers are required to *take account of these requirements and make provision, where necessary, to support individuals or groups of students to enable them to participate effectively in the curriculum and assessment activities* (DfEE, 1999, p27). Following this, specific guidance is provided for teachers on how to teach students with special educational needs, students with disabilities and students who are learning English as an additional language. We could also add to this list the needs of students who have been identified as gifted or talented who can often be unwittingly excluded in our classrooms.

In many respects, the challenges thrown up by the debate on educational inclusion find their resolution, or at least a partial resolution, in a declared commitment to creativity in teaching and learning. We will now consider how broadening your teaching style to encompass creativity can each help you teach your subject in a more inclusive way.

REFLECTIVE TASK
REFLECTIVE TASK

Making sure that you address the needs of all your students is a vital part of teaching. The inclusion materials summarised above are vitally important and contain much practical advice about how to teach your subject in an inclusive manner. These relate to all of your teaching, not just the work that we might identify as being especially focused on creativity. Spend a few minutes reflecting on the teaching that you have witnessed or done yourself. Ask yourself the following questions:

- How can my planning and preparation, particularly the setting of key learning objectives, really help meet the learning needs of all my students?

- What are the common approaches to differentiation in your subject area? How can these help create an inclusive learning environment?

- What approaches have you seen other teachers take to help support students with special educational needs, students with disabilities, students with English as an additional language or gifted/talented students?

- How can I best utilise the support of other adults in my classroom to assist me in providing for the diverse range of student needs that I will often face lesson by lesson?

Creativity and inclusive teaching and learning

Each individual plays out their little c creativity in a unique way, according to their talents, skills and aspirations. (Craft, Jeffrey and Leibling, 2001, p55)

As we have seen in Chapters 2 and 3, at the heart of teaching creatively and teaching for creativity is the creative teacher. Not many of us will be creative in the 'high creative' sense discussed earlier. But a personal commitment to a little c creative teaching approach is essential. What does this look like? How will it help address the individual needs of the students you are teaching? What exactly are the creative elements that will help you provide an inclusive educational environment for your students?

Develop good relationships with your students

Effective teaching is built on a constructive relationship between teacher and student. At the heart of the documentation summarised above are themes which require teachers to have a detailed knowledge of their students in order to respond to their individual needs and make effective provision for them. Creative teaching has the potential to generate a greater range of responses to these key issues. As Craft states, *one cannot be creative with respect to nothing* (ibid.).

Creative processes are as important as creative products

The creative teacher will realise that individual student needs are best supported and developed through an ongoing educational process that should be, at key moments, characterised by creative interventions by the teacher on behalf of the student. Teachers need to model a creative process in their own work in order to draw students into the inherent possibilities of their own creative processes. Increasingly, as we will see below, these creative interventions will be matched by similar creative responses by the student. It is imperative that teachers journey with the student on this creative process:

> Little c creativity involves not being satisfied with what already exists, but considering other possibilities, which may include ones we do not yet know about ... It may involve both problem-solving and problem finding. (ibid.)

Teaching and learning is a shared responsibility

This creative educational journey will be facilitated by a shared ownership of the learning and teaching process. The model of the teacher being the fount of all knowledge and sole provider of information is outdated and inappropriate as one seeks to generate this inclusive and creative educational environment. A model of creative teaching where the teacher is a facilitator of learning may be more appropriate. Certainly, the teacher and student will need to work together to identify and solve problems. The teacher will be required to assist the student in identifying possibilities that exist outside the realm of their current experience and lead them to a new awareness within a particular field of knowledge. Similarly, we should not be surprised if, in certain subjects at least, students surprise us with their own insights about creative possibilities.

Possibility thinking as a tool to encourage inclusive approaches to creativity

So what precisely can we expect from all our students in respect of creative processes and products? Given that, for the majority of the time, we would expect to see our students delivering P-creative work in response to our teaching, what are the precise attributes that this work will contain? A return to Craft's theory of little c creativity is helpful in addressing these questions and giving us a clear picture of the skills, knowledge and understanding that we can expect all students to develop.

As we discussed above, little c creativity has at its heart the notion of 'possibility thinking' or, in Craft's words, a commitment from students to asking the 'what if?' question in a variety of ways (Craft, Jeffrey and Leibling, 2001, p54). Craft's final part of her exposition on little c creativity gives us a list of attributes, qualities or features of little c creativity that helpfully illuminate a perspective of creative learning in light of the inclusion agenda. These include:

- **self-determination and direction;**
- **innovation;**
- **action;**
- **development;**
- **awareness of convention;**
- **risk;**
- **being imaginative;**

- **posing questions;**
- **play.**

We will consider each of Craft's identified features of little c creativity below. Each feature is followed by a simple definition and then a series of questions designed to help you think through how that particular feature might helpfully promote an inclusive approach to learning and teaching for creativity in your own subject.

Self-determination and direction

These are fundamentally necessary to enable personal route-finding at a variety of levels from the mundane to the significant.

Key questions:

1. To what extent do you allow students freedom to explore a particular subject area in a way that allows them to build on their own interests?
2. How can knowledge acquisition in your subject be structured in such a way that facilitates students' opportunities to take ownership over the learning process?
3. How can you manage that freedom in a way that avoids anarchy in the classroom but allows for individual expression and moves towards independent learning?

Innovation

Creativity must involve a degree of innovation. Creative outcomes may be at the level of ideas and not yet in the public domain for scrutiny.

Key questions:

1. What does it mean to be innovative in your own subject area?
2. How can opportunities for innovation be balanced against the inevitable acquisition of knowledge that all subject areas demand?
3. Are certain subjects just more innovative than others? What are the key creative areas in your subject?
4. Are certain students just more innovative than others? What are the skills, processes or abilities that students need to learn in order to be innovative in your subject area?

Action

Without some sort of action, even an idea cannot be creative.

Key questions:

1. How do you encourage students to be active in your lessons and demonstrate ideas?
2. Are these means inclusive enough to allow all students to communicate, demonstrate, rehearse and receive feedback on ideas?

Development

Innovation and action will lead inevitably to development. Little c creativity is about continual development on to a new 'place'.

Key questions:

1. Within your subject, what levels of innovation or action are you expecting your students to progress from and to?
2. How do you keep track of individual student progress in such a way that encourages their development and gives them individual feedback?
3. How can all students be encouraged to take ownership of the learning process and maintain this 'continual development'?
4. When and how should you intervene in this process of development, to assist or check that it is proceeding in a constructive manner?

Awareness of convention

Knowing that one has been creative with reference to previous convention (either one's own or that of a wider field).

Key questions:

1. How can students be encouraged to reflect upon the background knowledge of your subject in such a way that makes them aware of the possibilities for creative action?
2. Who makes the decision about which conventions are important, when and how they are presented and discussed?

Risk

The weighing of possible benefits and losses as outcomes are part of what entices students to take a risk or avoid it. Students need to be encouraged to take risks that matter.

Key questions:

1. How should you conceptualise risk in your subject?
2. How does the taking of a risk result in a creative outcome?
3. How is risk-taking rewarded or encouraged within your subject area?
4. Should you take risks in your own teaching? What would these look like? How would they facilitate an inclusive learning environment for your students?
5. Is failure valued as much as success in the teaching of your subject?

Being imaginative

Coming up with a possibility which is novel and unexpected by seeing more than is evident initially.

Key questions:

1. How can you allow space in your teaching for all students to begin to uncover for themselves more than is obviously apparent?
2. Generally, how will you be aware of the novel and unexpected outcomes students will uncover? Will their responses be mainly P-creative or H-creative?
3. For P-creative outcomes, how can you structure lesson content in such a way that all students will really feel as though they are discovering something new as if for the first time?

Posing questions

Posing questions is at the root of openness to possibility.

Key questions:

1. How do the questioning strategies outlined in Chapter 3 facilitate an inclusive teaching pedagogy in which all students' viewpoints are valued and encouraged?
2. Who asks the questions in your classroom? How can you encourage and develop your students' questioning skills to facilitate the creative process?

Play

Being open to playing with ideas and new possibilities/combinations is logically necessary for little c creativity.

Key questions:

1. What are the key ideas within your subject that students will need to play with?
2. How can these be structured in such a way that facilitates students' play with them?
3. How do we prevent students closing down ideas too soon and assist them in the process of playfully trying out new possibilities and combinations of ideas?

A SUMMARY OF **KEY POINTS**

> Creativity is not only possible but a desirable feature in the work of all your students.

> Craft's notion of little c creativity and Boden's H- and P-creative work are helpful ways of conceptualising the creative elements of your students' work.

> These concepts need to be applied within the context of the individualised learning and government documentation in each subject area.

> By analysing the creative process and its particular elements, a more inclusive educational environment can result within which your students can be treated as individuals, empowered accordingly and be encouraged to produce their own creative processes and products.

FURTHER READING FURTHER READING **FURTHER READING** FURTHER READING

Boden, M. (1990) *The creative mind: myths and mechanisms*. London: Weidenfeld & Nicolson.

Craft, A., Jeffrey, B. and Leibling, M. (2001) *Creativity in education*. London and New York: Continuum.

DfEE (1999) *The National Curriculum for England* (various individual subject documentation). London: DfEE.

8
Creativity and motivation

By the end of this chapter you should have:

- examined how motivation plays an important part in creativity for students and teachers;
- explored notions of extrinsic and intrinsic motivation and how these can help or hinder creativity in the classroom;
- considered a range of motivational attributes for creativity and begun to think how these will inform your future teaching.

This chapter will help you to meet the following Professional Standards for QTS:

Q1, Q2, Q12, Q19, Q25, Q27, Q28

Introduction

This book has promoted a view of creativity in the classroom that is holistic, in the sense that creativity is fostered and developed when a number of elements come together within a specific teaching or learning environment. The precise elements that are required are debated quite vigorously in the research literature, but we find Cropley's summary a useful starting point (Cropley, 2001, p144):

- the individual's creative potential;
- other psychological properties of the individual;
- aspects of the creative process such as divergent thinking;
- aspects of the environment such as the degree of risk that it will accept;
- special characteristics of the task itself such as its degree of definition;
- the nature of the desired solution such as the level of novelty that will be tolerated.

Cropley's summary is neatly divided into two main parts. The first part focuses on the individual, the second on the nature of a task or activity. The application of this is obvious and useful: *fostering creativity cannot be achieved by focusing on the individual person alone*. (Cropley, 2001, p145)

In our context of initial teacher education, we have taken this broader view and looked beyond the individual students' creative attributes. The focus in Chapters 2 and 3 was primarily on you as a teacher and how you teach creatively and for creativity. Chapter 4 moved the focus onto your students and how their learning could encompass, develop and improve through creative learning opportunities. In the following chapters we have considered a number of other facets of teaching and learning that affect how you might promote creativity in your classroom, including assessment processes (Chapter 5), the use of ICT (Chapter 6) and the need for educational inclusion (Chapter 7). Finally, before we come to our last chapter that will consider your future development, we will turn our attention to another vital element needed for creativity in the classroom: motivation.

Why creativity and motivation?

Creative engagement was enhanced where learning was pupil-led, that is where pupils had a sense of ownership of outcomes and were given a choice in the content and a voice in the expression of their work ...

Pupils responded better in activities where there was room for them to experiment and extend activity independently and where they were encouraged to articulate individual aims for their work ...

Pupil learning was motivated by the presence of 'expert' adults ...

Encouraging expression of a range of learning styles contributed to the personalisation and open-endedness of projects ...

Pupils can become far more highly motivated, confident and well-behaved while engaging in musical creativity ...

There was evidence that creative engagement improved learning behaviour, e.g. the use of multi-sensory creative activity, increased attention span and improved general alertness and behaviour of project children with profound special needs ...
(CARA, 2005, p13)

All of these comments are drawn from a series of reports from projects that delivered creative approaches to teaching and learning during 2005. The positive benefits from adopting these approaches included greater pupil engagement and response, motivation, increasing personalisation of learning, increasing confidence and better behaviour. By now, we hope that you can see the benefits of teaching creatively, teaching for creativity and creative learning. As we have said throughout the book, as you develop your teaching and gain more experience, you will begin to see the links between these three important concepts and the integrated pedagogical approach that develops will affect all aspects of your teaching. The chapters in the second half of this book have examined how this works out in a number of ways. Figure 8.1 shows how these themes relate to the ideas of creativity and motivation which are the focus of this chapter.

The NACCCE report proposed that teaching for creativity involves three key principles: encouraging, identifying and fostering. This chapter focuses on the first of these. It is about encouraging and motivating your students:

Highly creative people in any field are often driven by a strong self-belief in their abilities in that field. Having a positive self-image as a creative person can be fundamental to developing creative performance. Many young people and adults do not think of themselves as creative and lack the confidence to even take the first steps. Consequently, the first task in teaching for creativity in any field is to encourage young people to believe in their creative potential, to engage their sense of possibility and to give them the confidence to try.
(NACCCE, 1999, p90; my emphasis)

When we look to the wider research literature for clues about how students can be encouraged and motivated by and through teaching for creativity, the concepts of extrinsic and

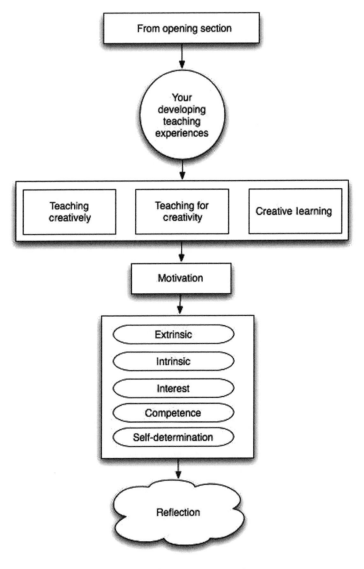

Fig. 8.1. Chapter 8: overview

intrinsic motivation are quickly identified and some vigorous debates ensue. We will explore some of these briefly below.

Models of extrinsic and intrinsic motivation

Developing classroom structures that support intrinsic motivation is an essential element in developing creativity in schools. (Starko, 2001, p320)

Many of the models of creativity found in the literature have a focus on motives and motivation. Historical studies of famous creative people often reveal that motivation plays a vital role in their continued success. Cox's work shows that geniuses such as Newton and

Darwin had a great degree of perseverance and motivation as well as extremely high intelligence (Cox, 1926). In the sporting area, one can easily realise that ability on its own is not a recipe for success. If, as Bayli points out, to become an elite sports-person you need to train for 10,000 hours over eight to twelve years then ongoing motivation is clearly going to be required (Bayli, 2006)!

Much of the research on creativity points to the centrality of intrinsic motivation. Intrinsic motivation is the desire to carry out an activity for the sake of the activity itself. Amabile's model of the creativity intersection and her research on intrinsic motivation and creativity is interesting (Amabile, 1989). According to her research, intrinsic motivation has three main requirements.

1. *Interest*. This is relatively obvious, but anyone is more likely to be motivated by something that has captured their interest rather than something of no perceived value.
2. *Competence.* The motivating effects of increasing competence in a particular domain are considerable. Students will seek out activities and persist in them for longer if they feel they are mastering something, particularly if they are doing this on their own (Amablie, 1989, in Starko, 2001, p143)
3. *Self-determination*. This moves students beyond the need for success in a particular activity. To be intrinsically motivated, they have to feel that they are pursuing the activity because they have chosen to do so. They have to feel that they are working on an activity, in a particular subject area, for their own reasons rather than for yours (Amabile, 1989, in Starko, 2001, p144).

Intrinsic motivation is contrasted with extrinsic motivation. In our context, extrinsic motivation could be associated with external rewards such as praise, prizes, grading, positive testing or even the avoidance of punishments. A significant portion of the research literature strongly supports the view that students can only be truly creative when they are intrinsically motivated. It is suggested that the use of extrinsic motivation can only shape their behaviour and lead to conformity to the expected outcomes of the teacher which, of course, is necessary to receive the award. In this context, conformity becomes the opposite of creativity.

Relatively recent research has begun to explore a more positive interpretation of extrinsic motivation in the classroom. Eisenberger and Armeli's (1997) work has shown that extrinsic rewards can lead to *enduring improvements even in a creative area such as music when children were rewarded for specific 'creative' behaviours such as incorporating unexpected elements or producing alternative possibilities* (Cropley, 2001, p62).

At a practical level of application, there has to be a balance in your teaching between extrinsic and intrinsic motivation. The research literature in these areas is complex and it is hard to draw conclusions. But we are happy to indicate that there seems to be a tenuous consensus that:

> *Intrinsic motivation is conducive to creativity; controlling extrinsic motivation is detrimental to creativity, but informational or enabling extrinsic motivation can be conducive particularly if initial levels of motivation are high.* (Amabile, 1996, p119)

Or, as Starko puts it more bluntly:

Intrinsic motivation is supportive of creativity. Some types of extrinsic motivation are harmful to creativity, some are not. Of course, our task is to determine which is which and how best to use them in classrooms. (Starko, 2001, p325)

So what would be the distinction between good and bad forms of extrinsic motivation in your teaching? One of the key distinctions from the research literature suggests that it is the extent to which the extrinsic motivational factors are controlling or informational:

Controlling extrinsic motivation is the driving force behind an activity, perhaps the only reason it is undertaken. Classrooms that operate under threat of tests and grades are centering on controlling extrinsic motivation. Praise that is doled out to good pupils without a clear indication of what they did well can have a similar effect ... Praise that gives pupils information about what they did well and enhances their sense of competence is less detrimental. The more obvious the external motivation, the more problematic it is. (Starko, 2001, pp325–6)

Craft, Jeffrey and Liebling (2004) extend this point and suggest that extrinsic motivation might be more beneficial early in the learning process, with intrinsic motivation taking over at a later stage:

Teachers can provide extrinsic forms of motivation, e.g. incentives or rewards, but it is also important that children are encouraged to develop intrinsic forms of motivation, e.g. curiosity. The former will aid the immediate acquisition of knowledge of skills at school, but the latter will sustain a person's interest in a field and encourage an individual to become a lifelong learner. Once children have developed or found their individual forms of intrinsic motivation, extrinsic motivation should be applied cautiously, as it might stifle creativity. (Craft, Jeffrey and Liebling, 2004, p23)

However you interpret the research literature, the manner in which you apply the models of extrinsic and intrinsic motivation will depend on the individual students and classes that you teach. You will have to draw on these ideas and see what does or does not work. This leads us on to the next question, what exactly should we be seeking to motivate in our students in order to encourage creativity?

RESEARCH SUMMARY RESEARCH SUMMARY RESEARCH SUMMARY RESEARCH SUMMARY

- Motivation features in most models of creativity within education.
- Motivation is normally characterised as either extrinsic or intrinsic.
- Intrinsic motivation is generally considered to be a virtue for creativity.
- There is no consensus about the benefits of extrinsic motivation for encouraging creativity.
- Teachers will need to make individual judgements about the precise benefits of extrinsic and intrinsic motivation for their students.

REFLECTIVE TASK
REFLECTIVE TASK

Think through the various forms of extrinsic and intrinsic motivation that you have seen at work in the lessons that you have taught or observed. What effect did these have on student motivation? Did they lead to more creative processes or products in your opinion? Have you been able to observe any links between creative activity and student motivation?

Motivation for creativity

In this final section we will be considering the features that are required to encourage a motivation for creativity. Firstly, we will focus on your students and, secondly, on you as their teacher.

Students' motivation for creativity

Drawing on a range of information, we can construct a list of attributes needed for creativity that we should motivate in our pupils:

> *The encouragement of attributes like risk-taking, independent judgement, commitment, resilience in the face of adversity and motivation will contribute to the development of children's creative potential.*
> (Craft, Jeffrey and Liebling, 2004, p23)
>
> *Other attitudes are important for creative development; these include high motivation and independence of judgement, willingness to take risks and be enterprising, to be persistent and to be resilient in the face of adversity and failure. These attitudes can be encouraged and nourished to varying extents in all young people, particularly if they are linked with the development of self-directed learning.* (NACCCE, 1999, p90)

Table 8.1 lists some of these attributes together with an application to your work as a trainee teacher.

Table 8.1 Motivation attributes for pupil creativity

Attribute	Application	Questions
Risk taking	Risk taking may not be a natural process for young teenagers who may be under a lot of peer pressure and depend heavily on group security. As they get older, teenagers may express a strong desire for independence and this could be an opportunity for you, as their teacher, to channel them towards creative activities. But be careful – you will need to ensure that loss, in terms of risk taking, is not seen as failure.	How should you structure your lessons to include elements of risk taking? How can you ensure that the potential gains or losses associated with taking risks do not equate to notions of success or failure?
Persistence, adaptability and resilience	There is always more than one way to solve a problem. Students should be encouraged to view and analyse problems in different ways and not to give up after initial attempts to solve them. Adapting the process and maintaining a resilient attitude until the problems are solved is important in order to achieve creative outcomes.	When you present new knowledge in your subject area, how can you present a range of alternatives and viewpoints? How can you encourage students not to give up when learning is difficult and little

apparent progress is being made?

How can you counteract the 'Done it, Sir!' attitude that some pupils bring to every task you set them?

Independence	Students need opportunities to identify their own interests within a subject and pursue these individually. However, this does not equate to you taking a backwards step in their learning process. These opportunities need very careful structuring and planning if they are to be successful.	Independent learning is fine, but how do you encourage thirty students to all follow their own interests, simultaneously, in a typical classroom environment? More positively, how can you use differentiation in your subject area to encourage independence in learning? What tips and techniques have you observed experienced teachers use to encourage individual student's interests?
Self-evaluation	Effective self-evaluation requires students to measure their efforts in some way. It will help them realise that creative products can be measured in some way by the standards of the day, even though there is often room for debate and differing interpretations of value. Encouraging approaches to self-evaluation will also help you with assessment for learning.	How can approaches to self-evaluation feed into assessment for learning? Whose standards should you use for the evaluation or assessment of your pupils' work? Where do your students get ideas about the standards of their work? How do the products of self-evaluation help you measure the value of your students' work through more formal assessment mechanisms?
Openness to new experiences	Seeking to move students out of their 'comfort zone' is a prerequisite for creative teaching and teaching for creativity. Nevertheless, it is not easy, particularly during their younger teenage years. Students will often seek your approval and reassurance when they are moving into new, as yet undiscovered, areas of the curriculum.	What are the best ways of introducing new subject knowledge to your students in a way that feeds their natural sense of enquiry? How can you provide the necessary reassurance for students through the structures and resources of your lesson rather than them always looking to you directly for approval?

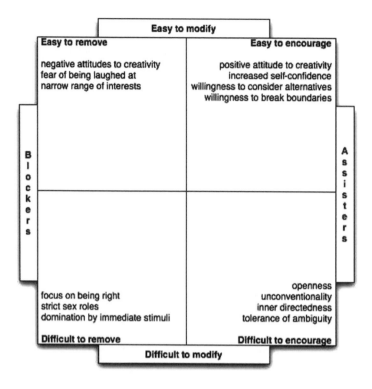

Fig. 8.2. Cropley's modifiers and blockers

The desire to motivate and encourage students' creativity is a genuine one amongst educators, but this is not without its difficulties:

> It is not difficult to imagine that knowledge, skills and abilities can be affected positively by training. Indeed the assumption that this is the case is at the heart of all educational procedures and institutions and it would be absurd to challenge it ... Experience in the classroom suggests that some aspects of personality and motivation are relatively easy to influence in a positive way whereas others are difficult to affect. (Cropley, 2001, p129)

Figure 8.2, drawn from Cropley's work (Cropley, 2001, p130), is a helpful reminder that in challenging motivational aspects of creativity we are dealing with the growth of students' personalities which consist of diverse traits that have developed through complex biological predispositions and environmental conditioning. We should be wary of overstating what we might be able to achieve or claiming too much credit when we appear to make progress with an individual student. Figure 8.2 shows Cropley's view of what is relatively easy to modify and encourage, together with what is more difficult.

Teachers' motivation for creativity

A vital influence in motivating your students towards creativity will be the demonstration of creativity in your teaching. We examined this in detail in Chapter 2. Here, we return to our exhortation to be a creative teacher and to share your creativity with your students at every possible opportunity.

Cowley's (2005) work demonstrates the importance of teachers sharing their own creativity with their pupils as a way of encouraging motivation. This can have many benefits and it is a worthy objective for every teacher. As we have seen in Chapter 2, an important part of teaching creatively is the engagement of creative skills in the act of teaching itself. Here, Cowley suggests that examples of creative work from your subject itself can be usefully shared with pupils. This has a number of benefits (Cowley, 2005, pp66–7):

1. It is fun and fulfilling for us as teachers.
2. It demonstrates that even teachers can be creative!
3. It presents a piece of ourselves to our pupils. This can be scary but ultimately rewarding.
4. It is a good leveller and places us in our pupils' position for a while.
5. It helps us understand the creative process that pupils will be going through and intellectualise it more rigorously.
6. We can use the experience as an opportunity to demonstrate how people respond differently to creative processes and outcomes and evaluate creative work in different ways.

PRACTICAL TASK PRACTICAL TASK **PRACTICAL TASK** PRACTICAL TASK **PRACTICAL TASK**

Think about the key messages of this chapter. As teachers, you have a vital role in inspiring students about your subject. You are also charged with maintaining and supporting their interest by sensitively handling the issues associated with extrinsic and intrinsic motivation. The following questions help you to think practically about how you do this in your teaching (adapted from Cropley, 2001, p155):

- How is the curiosity of your pupils stimulated, facilitated and supported?

- What opportunities are there within your teaching for pupils to become engaged in self-directed learning in order to support intrinsic motivation?

- How can you balance forms of extrinsic and intrinsic motivation in a way that promotes creativity rather than leading to conformity?

- How are your pupils' individual interests appreciated and supported?

- Is unnecessary repetition of knowledge and skills avoided in your teaching?

- How are pupil's questions accepted and expanded on in a constructive manner?

A SUMMARY OF KEY POINTS

> Motivation is an essential part of creativity.

> Intrinsic motivation plays the largest influence in maintaining and developing a student's work in your subject.

> Extrinsic motivation should be handled with care as it may lead to conformity rather than creativity.

> Teachers should try and promote a range of motivational attributes for creativity through their teaching.

> Teaching creatively is a vital part of sharing creativity and encouraging intrinsic motivation.

> Be realistic about what you can achieve in respect of an individual student's psychological development in this area.

REFERENCES REFERENCES **REFERENCES** REFERENCES **REFERENCES** REFERENCES

Amabile, T. (1989) *Growing up creative*. New York: Crown.

Amabile, T. (1996) *Creativity in context: update to The Social Psychology of Creativity*. Boulder, CO: Westview.

Bayli, A. (2006) *Long-term athlete development: trainability in childhood and adolescence; windows of opportunity, optimal trainability*. Online at: **http://coaching.usolympicteam.com/coaching/ kpub.nsf/v/2ltad04?OpenDocumentandClick=** (accessed 14 August 2006).

CARA (2005) *Building creative futures: the story of the Creativity Action Research Awards 2005*. London: Arts Council England and Cape UK.

Cowley, S. (2005) *Getting the buggers to be creative*. London: Continuum.

Cox, C. (1926) *Genetic studies of genius: the early mental traits of three hundred geniuses*. Palo Alto, CA: Stamford University Press.

Craft, A., Jeffrey, B. and Leibling, M. (2001) *Creativity in education*. London and New York: Continuum.

Cropley, A. (2001) *Creativity in education and learning: a guide for teachers and educators*. London: Kogan Page.

Eisenberger, R. and Armeli, S. (1997) Can salient reward increase creative performance without reducing intrinsic creative interest? *Journal of Personality and Social Psychology*, 72, 652–63.

NACCCE (National Advisory Council on Creative and Cultural Education) (1999) *All our futures: creativity, culture and education*. Sudbury, Suffolk: DfEE.

Starko, A. (2001) *Creativity in the classroom*. London and Mahwah, NJ: Lawrence Erlbaum Associates.

9
Your future development

By the end of this chapter you should have:

- begun to appreciate how teaching creatively, teaching for creativity and creative learning move from being discrete strategies to a unified pedagogical approach through reflection and ongoing teaching experience;
- understood that ideas relating to creativity in teaching and learning are in a constant state of development and redefinition and that you need to contribute to this debate;
- developed purposeful strategies, such as refinement and elaboration, that will lead towards reflective practice as the key to your development as a teacher;
- analysed 'reflection-in-action', 'reflection-on-action', reflecting on image and substance as keys to understanding the creative process of teaching and learning;
- learnt about some basic ways of understanding your own subjectivity;
- developed strategies that focus on your pupils as a source for reflective action.

This chapter will help you to meet the following Professional Standards for QTS:

Q1, Q7, Q8, Q29

Introduction

Throughout this book we have considered the ways in which you can teach various aspects of creativity in the classroom. We have provided you with ideas, suggested things to try out and given you plenty of things to think about. We have challenged you at this early point in your teaching career and, we trust, inspired you to start making your teaching 'creative' (in the fullest sense of that word) from the outset. We now turn to what you will need to do in the coming months and years as you move from being a trainee teacher, through your NQT year, and beyond into your teaching career.

Purposeful strategies towards redefining creativity in teaching and learning

Creativity is a dynamic and demanding component of contemporary education. All of the concepts, techniques and methods described in these chapters are active processes that require thought, deliberation and intervention through your teaching role. They do not happen by accident. We emphasised the importance of planning, and this will continue to be an important part of what you will be doing as a teacher once in post.

The concepts of teaching creatively, teaching for creativity and creative learning that we described and discussed in Chapters 2–4 are sets of discrete but complementary ideas, skills and techniques that are relevant for all teachers, in all schools and throughout all stages of a teaching career. Therefore many of the points that were made in those chapters will apply equally in your NQT year and beyond. But, as has been suggested throughout Chapters 5–8, as you continue gaining experience as a teacher we suggest that these three discrete concepts will merge and become part of your enriched pedagogy. This is why we have placed a box around these concepts under the second stage of our Figure 9.1

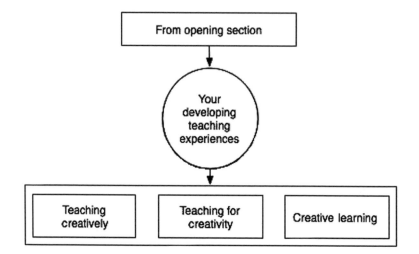

Fig. 9.1. Chapter 9: overview

As teaching creatively, teaching for creativity and creative learning begin to infiltrate and merge together within your own teaching style, you should expect to find yourself questioning what the descriptions mean and how they interact one with another:

> *Interrelationships between creative teaching, teaching for creativity and creative learning are still being explored and defined. Teachers and schools are, therefore, faced with the challenge of refining and elaborating the ways in which we can understand and enact these approaches to teaching and learning.*
> (Craft, 2005, p131)

Your understandings of creativity and how these outwork themselves out in the classroom will contribute to your overall knowledge of what is going on and how best teachers can take these ideas forwards. We have mentioned governmental and other initiatives that have put money into promoting creativity in schools. These developments are likely to increase in the coming years. We opened Chapter 1 saying how it is difficult to view creativity in anything other than a positive light. As the comment by Craft above shows, the terminologies we have been using are themselves subject to refinement and elaboration, and some of that needs to be undertaken by you, as you select and develop materials that will be suitable for *you* to use in *your* classroom with *your* pupils. Please do not fall into the trap of thinking what has worked for one teacher will automatically work for you! This is not the case, although we can always learn from each other's successes and failures.

The idea of refinement and elaboration is an important one for you to take with you in your planning, both now and in the future. As a student, and possibly as an NQT, you will often be involved with teaching from extant materials and presenting them to your classes. You will certainly want to have made a difference to these materials, but you will still be presenting, in many cases, other people's ideas. This is where refinement and elaboration need to take place, as:

> *A lesson that was written for another class in another school will not necessarily work elsewhere.* (Mills, 2005, p94)

After a few lessons you will begin to know your classes, and will know that a class is an *ad hoc* collection of individual pupils, each of which, as Gardner's (1983) work on multiple intelligence shows, has their own specific collection of strengths and interests. As you begin to understand this diverse community with their range of individual needs, you will be in a position to think about what you can take from published materials that will be of benefit and use to your own classes. It is likely that over the next few years more published ideas on creative projects, creative learning and teaching for creativity will become available, and it is important for you to think about the appropriateness of these materials for your context. After all:

> *[The] literal following of unsuitable material in published schemes arises because teachers do not understand what the publication is getting at, and think that this is their problem ... Published schemes of work need to be appraised confidently and critically by teachers – no matter how seemingly authoritative and definitive their source.* (Mills, 2005, p94)

Again, this leads to issues of refinement and elaboration. Where should you look for guidance and advice? Firstly, and most importantly, you should seek to reflect critically on *your* strengths and the needs of individual pupils within *your* classes. It is in this area that your ability to utilise structured approaches of reflective practice will be key. This area of *reflection*, particularly of undertaking purposeful and structured reflection, is an important area for your future development, and it is to that that we now turn our attention.

Evaluating teaching and learning

Learning to teach is a life-long process because teaching and learning are complex, dynamic and interactive processes that occur between individuals, individuals and particular institutions, and individuals and various resources and materials. In Chapter 6 we briefly examined Wertsch's (1998) notion of mediated action and how this relates to the use of ICT as a tool for teaching and learning. But mediated action can be applied much more widely that this. For example, *language is a cultural tool and speech is a form of mediated action* (Wertsch, 1998, p73). Analysing language use and speech is of vital importance for any teacher, and no doubt this is something which you have had to consider throughout your initial teacher education (and will continue to consider throughout your career). The essential point here is that teaching and learning are complex, dynamic and interactive processes that occur, in real time, in an 'instant' which cannot be easily repeated. While you may have a clear theoretical view of what these processes entail, it is also important to recognise the views that others hold, not least your pupils, and that theoretical understandings can be challenged through practice. Bruner's notion of folk pedagogy reinforces this point, emphasising the importance of understanding the potential conflicts that can erupt within a learning environment like a classroom if one is insensitive as a teacher to pupils' view of education:

You had better take into account the folk theories that those engaged in teaching and learning already have. For any innovations that you, as a 'proper' pedagogical theorist, may wish to introduce will have to compete with, replace, or otherwise modify the folk theories that already guide both teachers and pupils.
(Bruner, 1996, p46)

This is an important point that we will return to below. For now, it is clear that learning to teach is a gradual process that centres around the adoption of a complicated set of skills that will, at a basic level, develop over time. Furlong and Maynard (1995) have conceptualised the development of trainee teachers in the following five stages.

1. *Early idealism* – clear, if idealistic, views as to what sort of teachers they wanted to be.
2. *Personal survival* – idealism fades when confronted with classroom realities, and 'fitting in' becomes most important, especially with regard to behaviour management.
3. *Dealing with difficulties* – trainees begin to make sense of things and achieve a measure of classroom control.
4. *Hitting a plateau* – having found a way of teaching which 'works', more or less, a trainee sticks with it and does not deviate from it.
5. *Moving on* – trainees worked with tutors, supervisors and mentors, to understand that there was a need to change.

As you progress through your training you are likely to find yourself moving through these stages, and will need to develop your own ways of dealing with them.

Reflection-on-action and reflection-in-action

A key area for your future development will be the capacity to reflect on things you have taught, things the pupils have learned, and ways in which teaching and learning have taken place in your classroom. Schön (1983) wrote about *the reflective practitioner* and proposed two models: *reflection-in-action* and *reflection-on-action*. He described the former as reflection which takes place *during* an event; the latter as reflection which takes place *after* an event. It is likely that during your training you will be providing written evaluations of your teaching. These will continue in a different form into and beyond your NQT year. As a trainee teacher, it is most likely that you will be undertaking reflection-on-action, and thinking about, and describing, events which took place in your lessons. You will be considering what you did, what the pupils did and what you could do differently next time. This is all well and good and it is highly likely that you will learn from these experiences and reflections. Reflection-in-action is a more sophisticated skill that you are likely to develop later, but will become part of your own metacognition regarding the ways in which you teach. The development of your skills of reflection-in-action will be aided through the following exercises.

As you write your evaluations, the fact that you will begin by focusing on *teaching* is an inevitable consequence of your early development as a classroom practitioner. However, as time progresses you, and your tutors, supervisors or mentors, will become more concerned with your evaluations focusing upon your pupils' learning. In developing your practice with regard to creativity you will also be concerned with reflecting on creative processes and products. You will want to consider which ways of teaching creatively or teaching for creativity proved to be most successful and, importantly, *why* this was the case. It will be of little use thinking that something you and the pupils did was good if the conditions surrounding it were so unique as to be not replicable, or the converse, that a creative learning episode went badly from your perspective yet did so for matters which were totally unforeseeable.

Image and substance

Reflection-on-action and reflection-in-action are useful skills for you as a developing teacher both during your training, and continuing once you are in post. During the early stages of your teaching career you will, as we noted, be most likely to be reflecting on things which have happened. There is an inherent danger contained within the notion of reflection that you simply hold a mirror up to reality. This will show you *image* not *substance*. Part of your developing skill in reflection should be looking beyond the image and thinking about what else was going on in your classroom. This involves moving from description towards causation.

Teaching example – English lesson

Reflection 1

In this lesson the pupils were really poor, I tried everything, stood them up, sat them down, shouted at them, got them to work in silence, sent a pupil out; but still they didn't get anything done.

Reflection 2

It snowed during break. I knew from the moment I saw the first pupils arriving that they would need careful handling before we could do any work. Having had a word with the class teacher over break, I had quickly devised a starter which involved the pupils thinking of how many snow-related words they could that begin with the letters S-N-O-W, I started them off with 'slush' and 'November'.

Reflection as active process

These teaching examples show how reflection as an active process can help. If the teacher of Reflection 1 thinks through the issues, then hopefully they can come up with a strategy which can be useful in the future. The writer of the Reflection 2 has considered causation and has provided descriptions of circumstances which help explain *why* the events which happened took place. Building on this information, the next time an event like this occurs this teacher will be able to draw on this experience in a more constructive manner and act accordingly.

Reflection-in-action is a skill you will develop as you spend longer in the classroom. This process often seems invisible when observing established classroom teachers, and will soon become so much a part of your make-up that ultimately it will become seamless in your own practice too. Developing your capacity for reflection-in-action involves a degree of metacognition, as you will need to be thinking about what you are doing *as you are doing it*. Do not worry if there seem to be lots of other things to think about to start with! Ultimately this will become a natural part of your daily work.

PRACTICAL TASK PRACTICAL TASK **PRACTICAL TASK** PRACTICAL TASK **PRACTICAL TASK**

As a kick-start activity for yourself to begin the process of reflection-in-action, try planning two separate purposeful and relevant creative learning episodes for one of your classes, but do not decide which of them you will employ until the class has begun!

Creativity is, as we have discussed throughout this book, not something that you can clearly predetermine. Reflection after you have undertaken a creative project should focus on aspects that you can influence on future occasions and on how to deal with those over which you only have limited control. If the focus of your creative activity has been on *process*, then consider what aspects of the *doing* of the task went well, and try to account for *why* this was. It is human nature that you will also want to consider what did not go quite so well – again ask yourself *why* and, critically, what *you* could do about it next time you undertake this sort of activity.

Building on reflection

We have seen how reflective practice is central to effective teaching, particularly as you seek to develop your integrated approach to teaching creatively, teaching for creativity and creative learning (Schön, 1983, 1987; Watson and Wilcox, 2000). Reflection is generally recognised as a standard way in which teachers can *become better acquainted with their own story* (Conle, 2000, p51). The vast majority of initial teacher education courses place reflective practice at the heart of their work with trainee teachers, following the lead of QTS Standards such as Q7, the main focus of this chapter. As we have discussed above, while seeking to teach creatively, teaching for creativity and inspiring your pupils as creative learners it will be vital for you to engage in a structured process of reflection-on-action and reflection-in-action. In the following sections we aim to give you some principles, drawn from some research done by Kushner, Peshkin and others, on how this process of reflection can be enhanced, firstly by understanding more about your own subjectivity and, secondly, by prioritising reflection through your own pupils' voices.

Where do you find meaning in your teaching and your pupils' learning?

> *... One of the artifices of evaluation is to portray individuals but to invest them (and their lives) with meanings derived from the projects in which we observe them – like clothing dolls ... The increasing predilection for incorporating biographical accounts in evaluation does not necessarily advance our understanding of how innovations, for example, are extensions of the values and experiences of people. Rather, they tend too often to show people as extensions of innovations ... Instead of drawing a boundary around a project experience and reading individual lives within the context of the project, we need, just a little more often, to provide life experiences as contexts within which to understand educational projects.*
> (Kushner, 1993, p39)

Kushner's research methods are interesting, provocative and challenging. He urges us to reconsider what teaching might look like. In particular, he argues vigorously for the adoption of innovative approaches to evaluation as part of teachers' work. But this is not without its problems. As the above quote illustrates, evaluative practices often seek to invest meanings onto people's actions, words or work in an external way, rather than really seeking to understand them from the inside out. What might this mean for your teaching and the adoption of a process of reflection? Here is the above quote again, this time rewritten with an emphasis on teaching:

> *One of the artifices of reflections on teaching is to characterise teachers and pupils, investing them (and their lives) with meanings derived from the classrooms*

in which we observe them – like clothing dolls ... The increasing predilection for reflection through educational accounts of classroom practice does not necessarily advance our understanding of how teaching creatively, teaching for creativity or creative learning, for example, are extensions of the values and experiences of teachers and pupils. Rather, they tend too often to show teachers and pupils as extensions of these innovations ... Instead of drawing a boundary around a classroom experience and reading teachers' and pupils' lives within this context, we need, just a little more often, to provide life experiences as contexts within which to understand educational innovation. (after Kushner, 1993, p39)

Kushner's challenge to teachers is to seek to understand innovation in education through the context of one's own life experience. Kushner is well aware that such an approach is open to misunderstanding and the criticism of individualistic navel-gazing. But his writing boldly challenges us to take more account of individuals and their life history:

Programs are subject to context as their meanings and significance are subsumed within personal lives. (Kushner, 1993, p58)

In order to really understand how you can teach creatively, teach for creativity and understand how pupils can become creative learners, you have to understand where both you and your pupils are coming from. Howard Gardner described it like this:

We must place ourselves inside the heads of our students and try to understand as far as possible the sources and strengths of their conceptions. (Gardner, 1991, p253)

The focus on you as a teacher was explored in the part of Chapter 2 where we considered what you bring to your teaching role by way of wider life experiences and knowledge. More fundamentally, your own subjective beliefs or values about teaching, creativity and learning will affect your views of effective teaching and learning over the coming years. It will be vital that you come to understand the nature of this subjectivity in a clearer way. Peshkin's work is a key to generating this kind of understanding.

Developing a subjective *I*

Defining 'subjectivity' as *the quality that affects the results of observational investigation* (Peshkin, 1988, p17), Peshkin highlights the requirement for any teacher to be *meaningfully attentive* (ibid.) to their own subjectivity as they conduct and reflect on their teaching activities. Peshkin describes subjectivity as a *garment that cannot be removed* which has the capability to *filter, skew, shape, block, transform, construe, and misconstrue what transpires* (ibid.). His work goes on to helpfully demonstrate this process through the identification of six subjective '*Is*' that he perceived and reflected on during an extended piece of educational research at Riverview High School in California.

Peshkin describes each of these areas of his subjectivity in some detail. Table 9.1 contains a micro-analysis of the foundations of Peshkin's Is drawn from the text of his article.

Table 9.1 Peshkin's subjective *Is*

Peshkin's Is	Foundation	Key quote
Ethnic-Maintenance *I*	Pre-Riverview in his own religious background and beliefs	This is, of course, my Jewish I, the one that approves of my own retention of ethnicity.
Community-Maintenance *I*	Discovered through a sense of a place and its history	I felt this one in various places, perhaps nowhere more strongly than at Mario's Snack Shop where an important sense of community was perpetuated every day.
E-Pluribus-Unum *I*	All the before, in-between and after class times at Riverview High School	The visual impression of the school captivated me from the first time I went there to the last. I had never seen such diversity; indeed, it did not exist to the same degree anywhere else in the community. I saw students together in a way that I found wonderful.
Justice-Seeking *I*	Through observation of Riverview's denigration and inherent racism of neighbouring communities	Riverview's denigration distressed me ... Although feelings of distress helped focus my enquiry – a positive outcome – they could make me defensive in a way that would not facilitate my analysis and understanding.
Pedagogical-Meliorist *I*	Reflection on teaching from the back of a classroom	This emerged from seeking ordinary-to-poor instruction given to youngsters who would suffer, I imagined, as a consequence of that instruction.
Non-research Human *I*	The warmth of people's reception and welcoming in their community (including that felt by his wider family)	This softens one's judgement; its by product is affection, which tends to reduce the distance between self and subjects that scholars presume is necessary to learning and write about a person, place or institution.

There are number of important points here. Firstly, the foundations for Peshkin's subjective *Is* are drawn from a range of sources, including:

- his own belief and value systems;
- his experiences of a particular environment or place;
- his ongoing experiences of life within the particular school;
- the wider community and the relationships that he, and other members of his family, established within that community.

Secondly, Peshkin's subjective Is are powerful influences on his work as a teacher (and researcher). They frame his thinking and, on occasions, become a stumbling block to his understanding about a particular issue. He has to take time to work through these issues and reach a fuller understanding. But recognising their existence and seeking to understand their influence is a vital first step.

Finally, Peshkin's work is helpful in defining subjectivities in two ways: intrinsic and situational. Intrinsic Is are part of your personality and remain with you wherever you go. Situational Is are context-bound and change from place to place. These general distinctions allow you to consider your work in a number of different ways and on a number of different levels.

Reflecting through Peshkin's *Is*?

The process of reflection described above is, in one sense, personal and idiosyncratic. But there are implications and potential benefits for your teaching, particularly as you begin to work out the approaches to teaching creatively and teaching for creativity that we have outlined within this book. These are summarised briefly below.

Understanding your own subjectivities is the root of educational understanding

Peshkin's subjective Is are one useful strategy for helping us understand the root values that underpin our conceptions of education and their working out through our teaching. His notion of a 'situational I' extends this metaphor into particular times and places and is equally valuable. But as a first step, seeking an enhanced understanding of your own subjective Is can be tremendously enlightening as you seek to reflect on your own professional practice in the areas of teaching creatively, teaching for creativity and creative learning.

Reflective strategies are crucial at all stages of teaching – from initial teacher education throughout continuing professional development

As we have seen, systematic reflection is central to initial teacher education throughout the United Kingdom. Similarly, for specific moments (e.g. a particular collaborative educational event), a process of performance management or as part of an external course of study (e.g. a further degree), teachers are required to provide evidence of their ongoing, self-evaluation. While many of these triggers for reflection could be conceptualised as 'external', Peshkin argues for the promotion of 'internal' reflective thinking that underpins and has benefit for all stages of teaching.

Seek to counteract the 'busyness' culture and allow space for reflection

As teachers we are faced with a range of competing demands on our energy and time. It is often too easy to prioritise badly and dwell on the insignificant at the expense of the significant. As you move into a permanent teaching post, it will be vital that you place your own, and your pupils', experiences at the centre of any educational agenda. It is vital that you do not become so busy that the space for this kind of reflection is lost.

Nurture your pupils' voices and their perceptions of your teaching

Finally, who is the best judge of your teaching? Recent research by Finney has stressed the importance of the pupil voice in initial teacher education. He examined the relationships between teachers and learners and how this can promote learning when it is characterised by a healthy connection, interest and concern among teachers and learners.

Finney challenges us to consider where skills, understanding and knowledge come from. Do they come from external, nationwide programmes of curriculum reform? Key skills, knowledge and understanding are, in this sense, caught not taught. Or, in Finney's words:

> *Skills, knowledge and understanding, in this instant, are imminent to the life of the learner, the teacher and the subject.* (Finney, 2006, p4)

This is an ultimate goal of all reflective practice, but it depends on that all-important teacher–pupil relationship. Listening to what pupils tell you about your teaching can be challenging, but it is vital if you are to really get to grips with teaching creatively or teaching for creativity.

RESEARCH SUMMARY RESEARCH SUMMARY RESEARCH SUMMARY RESEARCH SUMMARY

Kushner teaches us that reflection needs to be established in, and drawn from, a detailed appreciate of the lives of teachers and pupils.

Peshkin shows how the development of a 'reflective eye' is situated within your own subjectivities. These are powerful influences on what you think might constitute effective teaching and learning. They will also affect how you approach the whole issue of creativity in education. You need to acknowledge these influences and come to understand them in order to reach a greater understanding of your own classroom practice at a more detailed level.

Internal reflective thinking should be part of your teaching at all stages, from initial teacher education through to continuing professional development. Make time and space for this at all costs!

REFLECTIVE TASK

Spend some time considering what your subjective Is might be and try to answer the following questions:

- Can you identify any intrinsic subjectivities that are part of your own personality?
- What about the situational subjectivities that perhaps you found emerging during a teaching practice or while visiting a particular school?
- Can you compare teaching experiences in different schools and reflect deeply on the particular reasons for success or failure within different pupils or classes?
- What about the 'lens' of reflection? How can you reflect on different levels and alter the focus of your reflection in a helpful way?
- How can analysing your own subjectivity help you to reflect more deeply on your own role, influence and personality within the classroom?

Listening to the pupil voice

There is a rising tide of research telling us that listening to the pupil voice is important (Rudduck et al., 1996; Rudduck and Flutter, 2004). We know, for instance, that ...

> *When talking directly about learning in the classroom ... pupils also have a lot to tell us that is worth hearing.* (Rudduck and Flutter, 2000, p85)

This seems to make it a logical part of the day-to-day work of the teacher to listen! We also know that ...

> *The student perspective is likely to be insightful, challenging and almost certainly engaging.* (Finney and Tymoczko, 2004)

When undertaking teaching and learning episodes that involve creativity, pupils will want to be involved, and will want to take some responsibility for their own learning and their own creative processes. They are also likely to be aware of where problems and difficulties might lie:

> *Pupils affirm the excitement of problem solving tasks and tasks that allow them to use their own ideas. They can often explain what levels of difficulty they find productive in different kinds of task.* (Rudduck and Flutter, 2000, p85)

Listening to what the pupils are saying forms an important element of formative assessment, as we saw in Chapter 5. What Rudduck and Flutter are saying though is that the pupils are able to articulate their interests and their difficulties. The task for you as the teacher is to transform what they are saying into action. This is an essential part of a assessment for learning, i.e. building on the information you are given to promote and facilitate creativity and learning for the pupils. This is most likely to be effected in dialogic feedback sessions with the pupils – after all there is little point listening to pupils' voices if you then ignore what they say to you!

The central role of formative assessment

Formative assessment, or assessment for learning, is therefore central to your understandings of what pupils are saying. However, properly used formative assessments go well beyond this. Earlier, we discussed reflection-on-action and reflection-in-action, and it is in these domains that your emerging assessment skills will need to be honed. Once you are in a full-time teaching role it becomes all too easy to rely on summative assessments to tell you what you need to know. However, having a bulging mark book alone does not make you a good teacher! You need to assess and evaluate your teaching and the ways in which your pupils are working. Undertaking and evaluating creativity projects and episodes needs to be done purposefully and with a degree of responsiveness. To do this properly is to undertake a process which is very much akin to a process of educational research called *action research*.

RESESEARCH SUMMARY RESEARCH SUMMARY RESEARCH SUMMARY RESEARCH SUMMARY

The origins of the notion of action research are not entirely clear, but in 1940s America, Kurt Lewin was discussing how undertaking action research was *proceeding in a spiral of steps, each of which is composed of planning, action and the evaluation of the result of action* (Kemmis and McTaggart, 1990, p8). This is the essential feature of action research, the notion of a spiral of four stages as shown in Figure 9.2.

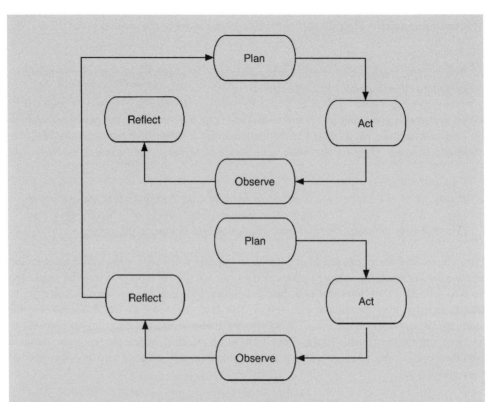

Fig. 9.2. Action research spiral

The four stages of action research identified in the diagram are as follows.

1. *Plan*. Here you devise the creative task or project which you and your pupils will be working on.

2. *Act*. In this phase the creativity work is done.

3. *Observe*. While the creative task or project is being done you observe and note what is taking place, undertake formative assessments, give feedback, evaluate actions and processes as they happen and undertake reflection-in-action as much as possible.

4. *Reflect*. In this stage you look back on what happened and undertake reflection-on-action.

Action research is normally considered to operate in a spiral, and so from the first occurrence there is a link to subsequent iterations, building up the spiral over time. Each subsequent 'rotation' builds on knowledge acquired from previous occasions.

Using the action research spiral as a model for reflection and evaluation serves a number of functions. It enables you to undertake structured reflection on creative work done by you and the pupils in your classes, and it enables you to learn from what you have done in order to do things differently on subsequent occasions. Using this model also enables you to tailor your work to different classes' responses – after all it is likely that each class working on a creativity project will do things in a different way so employment of this model will help you differentiate accordingly.

Baseline assessment

Before you can to begin to make progress with planning for your future development, you need to take stock of where you are. This is an important issue for you, as planning a route map for development needs a fixed starting point. To do this we recommend that you undergo a baseline assessment process with regard to various areas of your teaching practice. This will audit your current strengths in the areas of teaching creatively, teaching for creativity and inspiring pupils to creative learning throughout your training to this point.

REFLECTIVE TASK

Creativity audit

Using the 'route map' that we have been referring to throughout this book as a template, let us now consider where your personal strengths and weaknesses lie with regard to each of the major areas we have discussed. Table 9.2 takes you through *teaching creatively, teaching for creativity* and *creative learning* concepts, and asks you to plot where you feel you are by ticking the box in the four right-hand columns as appropriate. Areas where you are less confident are those which you can work at developing. As with meeting the QTS standards, you need to identify where you can improve and not just 'play to your strengths' all the time.

Table 9.2 Personal audit for teaching creatively, teaching for creativity and creative learning

Area of concern	Brief description	I have not done this yet	I have done this at least once	I am fairly confident in this area	I am very confident in this area
Teaching creatively					
Being an inspiration	Modelling enthusiasm				
Knowing your subject	Having a command of the area you are teaching				
Carry on learning	Keep yourself up to date with developments				
Making connections	Forming links, and helping your pupils do the same				
High expectations	Trying to get the best from your pupils				
Stimulate curiosity	Encouraging pupils to think 'outside the box'				
Being encouraging	Giving support, and fostering a 'can do' mentality				
Allowing time	... for pupils to work independently, and in groups				
Teaching styles	Knowing which style to use when, and developing your own				
Teaching for creativity					
Planning	Thinking through issues, short, medium and long term				
Questioning	Developing your skill in questioning to take the pupils forward				
Types of knowing	Developing 'knowing that' and 'knowing how to'				

Area of concern	Brief description	I have not done this yet	I have done this at least once	I am fairly confident in this area	I am very confident in this area
Group work	Enabling the creative process to be distributed among individuals				
Learning metaphors	Are your pupils 'acquiring' or 'participating'?				
Creative learning					
Process and product	Knowing which is the focus				
Experiential	Nurturing learning through doing				
Cross-curricular	Forging links between subjects and areas				
Imagination	Encouraging thinking				
Skills	Developing abilities				
Nurture/development	Doing is as important as regurgitating facts				
Enabling conditions	'Hope for success, plan for failure'				

Obviously some skills will be stronger than others. You will have been planning, for example, throughout your training and may feel particularly confident in this area. You will have been developing your skills at questioning, and will hopefully have a good knowledge of your subject. Try to think of these areas with specific reference to creativity and what you have done that would fall under one of these headings.

Table 9.3 Personal audit for assessment, inclusion, new technologies and motivation

Area of concern	Brief description	I have not done this yet	I have done this at least once	I am fairly confident in this area	I am very confident in this area
Assessment					
Process/product	Which are you assessing and why?				
Feedback	Practise making meaningful comments				
Target setting	Are they SMART?				
Authenticity	Are you clear about the rationale for what is being done?				
Group work	How do you assess knowledge which is socially constructed?				
Connecting strands	Using formative assessment to tell you and the pupils what to do next				
Valuing the verbal	What you say matters it is formative assessment				
Managing/recording	What happens to what you say? What happens to work you mark?				
Inclusion					
Little c creativity	Do you understand how little c creativity can democratise creativity and lead to an inclusive learning				

Area of concern	Brief description	I have not done this yet	I have done this at least once	I am fairly confident in this area	I am very confident in this area
	environment in your classroom?				
P- and H-creativity	Can you spot P- and H-creative responses in the work of your pupils?				
Learning challenges	Can you design suitable learning challenges that differentiate appropriately and give all pupils the chance of success?				
Diverse needs	Do you understand your pupils' prior experiences of learning and plan your lessons in full knowledge of their diverse needs?				
Overcoming barriers	Are you aware of the various requirements for supporting pupils with SEN, disabilities, EAL or specific gifts or talents?				
Inclusive teaching	Have you established good relationships with your pupils that facilitate the opportunities for creative teaching and learning?				
Inclusive learning	Is the learning process shared between yourself and your pupils? Are you encouraging and supporting your pupils towards educational independence as their diverse needs permit?				
Possibility thinking	Analyse how the features of possibility thinking apply within your subject. Can you structure lessons to facilitate the features of possibility thinking for all pupils?				
New technologies					
Mediated action	Understanding the links between technologies and teaching/learning tasks				
Controlling	Can you explain how pieces of hardware or software take control over the teaching/learning process?				
Interfering	How does ICT interfere in the teaching/ learning process beyond simply controlling you or the pupil?				
Limiting/facilitating	Can you choose pieces of ICT that best suit the teaching/learning context to facilitate the chances of successful outcomes?				
Motivation					
Extrinsic	Do you appreciate the balance that is				
Intrinsic	required between extrinsic and intrinsic motivation? Have you worked through the issues regarding which would be best, and when, within your subject?				

Area of concern	Brief description	I have not done this yet	I have done this at least once	I am fairly confident in this area	I am very confident in this area
Interest	Have you considered ways of ensuring that your pupils remain interested in your subject?				
Competence	How do pupils know they are succeeding in your subject? How do you reward, encourage or recognise increased levels of competence?				
Self-determination	How can you structure teaching and learning activities in such a way that encourages intrinsic motivation by generating a feeling of self-determination in your pupils?				

In Table 9.3 we consider material from the central chapters in the book, and how you rate yourself in the areas of assessment, inclusion, use of new technologies, and motivation. Again, think back on your experiences, and rate them accordingly.

A SUMMARY OF **KEY POINTS**

> Your period of initial teacher education has been a challenging one.

> There is no doubt that you have come a long way during this period. There will have been successes and failures, high points and low points. At times you may well have questioned why you were doing it and at other points you will have felt like it was the best job in the world!

All of the feelings above will continue throughout your teaching career. No one is the perfect teacher. We are all learning. Throughout this chapter we have stressed the importance of you reflecting on your own work through a range of processes and techniques. This is particularly important as you seek to develop a teaching style that promotes creativity, whether it be in your own role (teaching creatively), for your pupils (teaching for creativity) or exhibited in their work (creative learning). There is no simple methodology by which you can put these into practice, but we have worked through ideas, strategies, and theories which will help you. Teaching for creativity, teaching creatively and nurturing and fostering creative learning are not aspects of your professional practice which will become humdrum and mundane – by their very nature their outcomes will be unforeseeable. In a world where means and ends are becoming increasingly prescriptive creativity offers a breath of fresh air for your and your pupils. Enjoy!

REFERENCES REFERENCES **REFERENCES** REFERENCES **REFERENCES** REFERENCES

Bruner, J. (1996) *The culture of education*. Cambridge, MA and London: Harvard University Press.

Conle, C. (2000) Narrative inquiry: research tool and medium for professional development. *European Journal of Teacher Education*, 23 (1), 49–63.

Craft, A. (2005) *Creativity in schools – tensions and dilemmas*. Abingdon: Routledge.

Finney, J. (2006) Richer learning, poetic thinking and music understanding. *NAME Magazine*, 6 (18), 2–4.

Finney, J. and Tymoczko, M. (2004) *Secondary school students as leaders: examining the potential for transforming music education*. Online at: **http://www.isme.org/article/articleview/254/1/17/**

Furlong, J. and Maynard, T. (1995) *Mentoring student teachers – the growth of professional knowledge*. London: Routledge.

Gardner, H. (1983) *Frames of mind*. London: Heinemann.

Gardner, H. (1991) *The unschooled mind*. New York: Basic Books.

Kemmis, S.E. and McTaggart, R.E. (1990) *The action research planner*. Victoria, Australia: Deakin University.

Kushner, S. (1993) One in a million? The individual at the centre of quality control. In Elliott, J. (ed.) *Reconstructing teacher education: teacher development*. London: Falmer Press, pp39–50.

Mills, J. (2005) *Music in the school*. Oxford: Oxford University Press.

Peshkin, A. (1988) In search of subjectivity – one's own. *Educational Researcher*, 17 (7), 17–22.

Rudduck, J. and Flutter, J. (2000) Pupil participation and pupil perspective: 'carving out a new order of experience'. *Cambridge Journal of Education*, 30 (1), 75–89.

Rudduck, J. and Flutter, J. (2004) *How to improve your school: giving pupils a voice*. London: Continuum.

Rudduck, J., Chaplain, R. and Wallace, G. (1996) *School improvement: what can pupils tell us?* London: David Fulton.

Schön, D. (1983) *The reflective practitioner*. Aldershot: Academic Publishing.

Schön, D. (1987) *Educating the reflective practitioner: toward a new design for teaching and learning in the professions*. San Francisco: Jossey-Bass.

Watson, J.S. and Wilcox, S. (2000) Reading for understanding: methods of reflecting on practice. *Reflective Practice*, 1 (1), 57–67.

Wertsch, J. (1998) *Mind as action*. New York and Oxford: Oxford University Press.

Index

Added to a page number 'f' denotes a figure and 't' denotes a table.